THE RHYTHM INSIDE

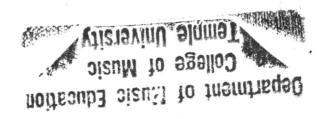
PAtgR8674047-B

THE RHYTHM INSIDE

CONNECTING
BODY, MIND, AND SPIRIT
THROUGH MUSIC

Julia Schnebly-Black, Ph.D. and
Stephen Moore, Ph.D.

RUDRA PRESS
Portland, Oregon

Rudra Press
PO Box 13390
Portland, Oregon 97213
Telephone: 503-235-0175
Telefax: 503-235-0909

*The authors and publisher disclaim any liability or loss, personal or otherwise,
resulting from the information and exercises in this book and compact disc.*

Cover and text design by Bill Stanton
Cover photography by Barry Kaplan
Composition by William H. Brunson Typography Services

Library of Congress Cataloging-in-Publication Data

Schnebly-Black, Julia.
   The rhythm inside : connecting body, mind, and spirit through music /
by Julia Schnebly-Black and Stephen F. Moore.
       p.   cm.
   ISBN 0-915801-68-X (alk. paper)
   1. Eurhythmy   2. Musico-callisthenics   I. Moore, Stephen F.,
1955–   .   II. Title.
MT22.S36 1997
780′.71— dc21   96-53670
                                                              CIP
                                                              MN

DEDICATION

To the many people who generously contributed insights from their personal lives so that this book could come to be.

ACKNOWLEDGMENTS

Special thanks go to the staff of Rudra Press: Karen Kreiger, Publisher, who caught the vision and set the process in motion; Ellen Hynson, Managing Editor, and Lorraine Millard, Developmental Editor, whose dedicated assistance helped give shape and proportion to what were sometimes unwieldy ramblings; Sarah Fahey, Marketing Director, who suggested the possibility of the book; and Bill Stanton, Art Director, whose designs have enhanced the appearance of the book. We also acknowledge Pat Moffitt Cook, Coordinator of the Healing with Sound and Music Series, who supervised the production of the CD.

The students in our 1996 summer Dalcroze Training Program at the University of Washington patiently repeated the exercises for the CD while we refined the commands. Thanks to them for their enthusiastic participation. We also thank the Jaques-Dalcroze Institute in Geneva, Switzerland for generous cooperation in helping us research remembrances from people who knew and studied with M. Jaques-Dalcroze.

CONTENTS

❦

FOREWORD

This book evolved from a Eurhythmics workshop held during the Western Regional Music Therapy Conference in Spring 1995. Attending the workshop were two staff members from Rudra Press who were deeply impressed with the potential Eurhythmics showed for profound effects on integrating body, mind, emotion, and spirit in our lives. Envisioning a new volume for Rudra's Healing with Sound and Music Series, they proposed that the authors share the joyful gifts of Eurhythmics by creating a work that would allow anyone, whether musically trained or not, to understand and apply the unique benefits of the Eurhythmics method of study.

With this book, we endeavor to show how Eurhythmics helps us appreciate the music we all have inside us, and how experiencing this inner music can strengthen and heal us physically, mentally, and spiritually, while giving us new self-confidence in our daily activities.

Across the world, Eurhythmics teachers and practitioners frequently discuss their responses to working with Dalcroze Eurhythmics—they speak of joy, increased concentration, heightened awareness, finer sensitivity, flow, openness, and balance. These universal reactions to this method of musical awareness encouraged us to explore *how* the practice of Dalcroze Eurhythmics not only enhances musical development but also exerts a much broader influence in people's lives. This book integrates two different fields of self-exploration and learning—the Eurhythmics body-movement approach to the study of music and the psychological study of human behavior.

Eurhythmics experience does not relate neatly to the phases of human behavior described by psychologists. For example, we find we cannot describe a Eurhythmics activity under the category of "perception" without also considering the role of "attention;" or we cannot speak of "attention" without also referencing "memory." These processes and connections weave together to form an intricate tapestry that is developed and refined through the practice of Eurhythmics.

At the International Congress of Eurhythmics held in Geneva in 1995, we personally interviewed many participants, including internationally recognized leaders in the Eurhythmics field; through the mail, we gathered additional interviews from people living around the world. (The interview respondents are listed in the Appendix.) Despite the wide differences in cultural, educational, and musical backgrounds between practitioners (both teachers and students), we found the amount of shared experience to be remarkable. We attempt to synthesize this range of experience in this book.

In our discussion of the writings of Emile Jacques-Dalcroze, the founder of Eurhythmics, we encourage readers to keep a certain perspective in mind. Remember that much of his writing developed during the 1920s, when the release from the first World War carried a euphoria about being "done with war." Hope ran high for evolution of humans into creatures of light and joy, full of consideration for the common good and sensitive to the aesthetic aspect of life. Dalcroze died in 1950, still holding fast to his bright vision for humanity. When Dalcroze declares that there would be no more worldy discord if everyone participated in Eurhythmics, he may sound unreasonably optimistic. But then again, since we have not tried, who knows?

We hope this book and its companion CD provide an accessible and rewarding way for you to explore this joyful method of developing your potential to creatively connect body, mind, and spirit in everyday living.

PREFACE

Healing with sound and music is a rapidly growing field, embracing music medicine, sound healing, music therapy, and non-Western music-centered therapeutic techniques. To these, we add music education and music performance, for it is by combining learning and performing in homes, schools, and community organizations that development toward wholeness is stimulated. For people of all ages, sensory integration is best supported and expressed by linking auditory stimulation and body movement.

This has been dramatically demonstrated by Switzerland's most celebrated musician and educator Emile Jaques-Dalcroze. He developed a system of rhythmic education using bodily movements to represent musical rhythms. He called this "Eurhythmics," from the Greek word meaning "good flow." Dalcroze Eurhythmics is designed to deepen awareness of musical rhythms in the body, thereby creating harmony between the body and the mind. The original goal to teach musicians and performers to really *know* music through their emotions, bodies, and minds, has extended way beyond pedagogy and musical mastery. In fact, it can become a well designed road to total well-being and spirituality.

Music educators find it imperative to understand the Eurhythmics method. Throughout the world, the subject is required coursework for graduate programs in music theory and composition. One of the leading teachers and masters of Eurhythmics is Julia Schnebly-Black, called a "gem" by all her colleagues. I had the pleasure of meeting her in August 1996 when we produced this book's companion CD in a Seattle recording studio. Ms. Black and her co-author, gifted pianist and instructor Stephen Moore, were teaching a summer Eurhythmics workshop at the University of Washington at the time.

For the CD, Julia and Stephen narrated and performed each exercise live to communicate in the simplest way with the listener-reader. The authors took great care to ensure no directions were omitted; each musical phrase was expressed and explained through physical gesture, stepping or clapping the beat, and breathing in response to rhythm. It was clear that these deceptively simple movements regenerate our deep collective responses to music and rhythm—keys to unlocking our emotions, thoughts, and healing potential.

"Good flow" is necessary for good health and communication. Dalcroze created a method to harmonize our energetic systems, expand our awareness, and enhance our enjoyment of daily life. *The Rhythm Inside* represents the authors' evolution of the Dalcroze tradition. They offer a practical and graceful teaching of the Eurhythmics method, a lifelong invitation for self-exploration and better health.

Pat Moffitt Cook
Healing with Sound and Music Series Coordinator

CHAPTER ONE

INTRODUCTION TO EURHYTHMICS

Imagine a Eurhythmics class ready to begin. The students prepare themselves—their bodies move into position, spines elongate, heads lift, shoulders relax, knees bend slightly, and senses heighten. The weight-bearing leg moves slightly forward, while the other foot lightly touches the floor behind. Seeing the attentive students ready to listen and move, the teacher gives a voice command—"Ready ... and go," and with music accompanying them, the class begins to move. Within each student, a transformation in taking place: Music is becoming movement.

As the sound vibrations travel through the air and enter the ear, the aural system transmits them to specific areas of the brain for processing. Information about the body's arrangement in space and the state of its musculature (relaxed or tense) comes to the brain simultaneously through the proprioceptive system. The visual sense carries images of the teacher's hands reaching toward the piano keyboard. The complex flow of internal messages moving along different branches of the nervous system operates similarly in anyone who must perform with precision and skill—a violinist, a tennis player, or a surgeon.

Dalcroze Eurhythmics was first developed to improve musicianship, but it was soon recognized that its practice could bring many benefits to daily living. As you read this book, you will learn how the Dalcroze method, taught at music and performance schools worldwide, can become part of your own self-exploration to help you increase your perceptions and awareness, focus your attention, and enhance your ability to improvise and respond creatively in situations of all kinds.

Exercises used in Eurhythmics are discussed in Chapter 8 and included on the accompanying compact disc; they will give you a taste of how this discipline opens up new worlds of sensitivity to yourself and your environment. We sincerely hope you can bring the knowledge, growth, and joy that Eurhythmics offers into your own life.

To begin our exploration, we might watch a group of four-year-olds move in a Eurhythmics class. We see that they are alert, involved, and having a good time. After walking on tip-toe to the accompaniment of light graceful music from the piano, they may suddenly jump when the music changes, or take long heavy steps when they hear another rhythm. They are learning to listen carefully and to react with precision. They are also learning to be a cooperative part of a group when, for instance, they take turns tapping a drum. Sometimes they can tap the drum softly with one finger and other times use the whole hand to make a powerful sound! They are becoming aware of the range of power in their bodies, and they are learning self-control. These activities are typical of Eurhythmics classes, where children not only learn about the qualities and characteristics of music but also learn a great deal about themselves and their environment.

A Eurhythmics class in a retirement home may find students in various states of health. Even those in wheelchairs move their shoulders in time to music, stopping quickly when the music stops and starting again when the music resumes at some unpredictable moment. They listen carefully, alert, alive, enjoying the game of "keeping up with the music." This musical challenge is exhilarating; it renews self-confidence, arouses a sense of fun, and builds a feeling of community.

Picture a group of adults at a music conservatory, all trained musicians, walking around a room in time with the music. They express the quality of the music by their manner of walking—light, graceful, forceful, tentative, or full of exuberance. They may clap their hands on every other step, then at a command, quickly change their clap to every third step, or fourth or fifth, according to the teacher's call. Later they may face each other in pairs, holding a hand drum between them, and tap rhythmic patterns for the other to echo, changing from groups of two beats to three or four, following the teacher's quick-fire instructions. Here is a challenge again—alertness expressed in precise movement that is molded by musical feeling. This, too, is a Eurhythmics class.

The word "Eurhythmics" derives from the Greek word Eurhythmy meaning "good flow." Musicians strive for this flow when performing. The ancient Greeks also used the term Eurhythmy to refer to the good form of an athlete in action or even the pleasing shape of a statue. When flow is missing, we say, "That athlete is off his game," "I do not like that statue," or "That architecture is fragmented." In a musical performance we say, "The music did not move me."

Eurhythmics is also the name of an approach to music learning developed by Emile Jaques-Dalcroze (1865–1950). This approach develops musical perception, increased awareness, improved attention, and greater control of musical expression. A Swiss educator, composer, and author, who spent most of his career in Geneva, Dalcroze developed Eurhythmics as a way to help his students "find the flow." He encouraged his students' musicality and bolstered their confidence by having them move their entire body to specific musical exercises.

At the Geneva Conservatory, Dalcroze began to experiment with new ways of teaching music to his students. His primary aim was to create a more effective way to involve musicians in their music; as his work progressed, he became aware that the results of this technique went well beyond the goal of training musicians to play better. There was a powerful influence on the total well-being of his students. This approach not only improved his student's musicianship—it touched their lives: encouraging the shy, balancing the awkward, bringing control to the impulsive and sensitivity to the unaware. Dalcroze eventually saw his work as a means to the healthy, balanced development of individuals.

Dalcroze's understanding of human behavior was so acute that the teaching procedures he invented tapped the innermost resources in every person. He discovered ways to harmonize the body's sensory systems, the emotions' evocative influence, and the mind's memory and creative functions. He observed that when these three aspects of human behavior were all well exercised, people naturally came into balance. They became at ease with themselves and with others. When internal communication flowed effortlessly between body, mind, and spirit without interference, the level of performance, insight, and creativity soared.

The unification of body, mind, and spirit was the cornerstone of Dalcroze's vision and the foundation of his teaching principles. Today we can appreciate how well his principles hit the mark. Recent research in human behavior shows how interdependent our health is on the cooperative functioning of the whole body—brain, sensory systems, organs, muscles, and the elusive mind and spirit.

Emile Jaques-Dalcroze: A Brief Biography

Switzerland's most celebrated music educator was born in Vienna in 1865. In 1875, Dalcroze's parents returned to their homeland of Switzerland and settled in Geneva. Dalcroze attended both the College and Conservatory of Geneva. Later in life, he wrote how his early experiences as a student affected his desire to make reforms in the field of education:

> I often suffered from the fact that the teachers weren't seeking the spiritual, nervous, or emotional states of their students... Not a word on the sonorities, on the melodies, the harmonies, the dynamic and temporal sonorities, not of emotion, not of style, no citations of beautiful works, no music[1]... These are the memories of my infancy and adolescence that put me on the path of pedagogical study.[2]

After graduation from the Geneva conservatory in 1883, Dalcroze left for Paris to pursue a performing career as a tenor. Talented in both the dramatic arts and music, he was torn between the two. He chose to combine his two interests by composing principally for the musical theater and integrating music and movement in his pedagogical method.

Returning to Geneva in 1886, he met the conductor and composer Ernest Adler, who offered him a post as his assistant conductor in a theater in French Algiers. Emile accepted this post, which proved to be one of the most fortuitous moves of his career. He writes:

> I was directing an orchestra of native musicians. Whereas the music I was teaching them was in quadruple time, the cymbal players were in quadruple time, and the flutes in triple time.

It was impossible to inculcate our methods into them. To teach the notation of our meter, I had the idea of interpreting each beat with a gesture.[3]

Dalcroze made several other discoveries that further impacted his teaching. He was impressed by how comfortable the native Algerians were with odd meters. These involved, for example, five- and seven-beat time. The Algerians also naturally adapted to irregular changes in meter and had a remarkable sense of accelerando and ritardando. He reasoned that these rhythmic sensitivities could become natural to musicians in Western Europe if they were cultivated in students at an early age. Philosophically, he conceived of the Algerians' performance of rhythm as representative of a deeper human impulse to express the irrational nature of emotion and feeling. He believed that incorporating these irregular rhythms into his teaching would heighten students' awareness of their inner sentiments.

In 1887, Dalcroze returned to Vienna where his studies with Adolf Prosnitz led him to the belief that improvisation should command an important place in music education. Improvising was a way to validate the student's thoughts and feelings. Rather than the teacher imposing a correct way of playing, the students learned to teach themselves. The teacher acted to guide them toward inventing their own techniques and experiences.

In 1892 Dalcroze was asked to fill the position of Professor of Theory and Solfege (sight singing from written music) at the Geneva Conservatory. At this time he envisioned the pedagogical importance of Eurhythmics, but it was his work at the Conservatory that convinced him of its necessity. He noticed that even the most gifted students in ear-training did not perform with enough musical expression and, thus, he felt their training incomplete. By 1900 he had incorporated ideas of phrasing and nuance into his Solfege classes and by 1903 had introduced physical exercises to accompany sight-singing.

At first, Dalcroze's new ideas met with fervent opposition from the faculty and public. In an attempt to counter this opposition, he held an open demonstration to encourage the acceptance of his teaching method. He wrote:

> Following the first demonstration, one of the members of the committee cried out, "You, Monsieur Jaques, are in the process of reviving the worst spectacles of Latin decadence."... Doctors reproached me, claiming that my exercises provoked a great fatigue; choreographers discussed the lack of technique; musicians remarked with disfavor on the use of unequal beats and measures and the establishment of form based not on the length of notes but on the weight of sonorous elements ... As for the parents, they judged the costumes completely unseemly and thought that the students should attain their majority before daring to remove their stockings.[4]

Due to the lack of support at the Geneva Conservatory, Dalcroze left Switzerland in 1910 to pursue an offer to teach in Hellerau, Germany (where a school was being erected according to his educational wishes.) The developers of this new school, a manufacturing family named Dohrn, planned much more than a degree-granting institution. Their intent was to build a Utopian city whose ideal was to find individual self-worth through the study of rhythm. For them the word "rhythm" had universal meaning. It alluded to the rhythm in the human body (the circulatory system and the breathing), rhythm in the human environment (movement in music, in art and architecture, of machines), and rhythm in nature (movement of animals, of plants, of tides, of light, or of seasons).

The buildings themselves reflected this philosophy. The main performance hall contained lighting booths, mobile screens, movable ramps, stairs, and walls that demonstrated the continuously changing aspect of rhythm. Many of these novel ideas, disseminated by students, revolutionized theater during the century.

We can observe some of the repercussions in modern dance and Broadway theater. The following words by Dalcroze, written in a letter to Wolf Dohrn, express his vision:

> In Berlin [Dalcroze had developed followers there] it is a matter of music only, of plastique also without a doubt, but above all, preparation for the art. Whereas, at Hellerau, it's a matter of creating an organic life; to harmonize the country and its inhabitants, thanks to a specialized education; to create through rhythm a moral and aesthetic architecture identical to that of your buildings; to elevate music to the heights of a social institution and prepare a new epoch.[5]

With the outbreak of war in 1914, Emile signed a petition criticizing the German war effort. That action forced him to leave the country. He returned to Geneva where the city welcomed him back by raising money for his school, the Dalcroze Institute, which still remains the center for the study of Eurhythmics. Continuing to teach at the school until his death in 1950, Dalcroze spent much of the next thirty-five years spreading the word of his method through writing and travel. He made several important trips to London, Paris, and Dresden in the 1920s, attempting to maintain a universal consistency to his method which was being taught by his students.

In 1929 Dalcroze returned to Germany with the intent "to reestablish the truth of my teaching. Eurhythmics has become [there] a technical science of the body. I want to reestablish the integrity of my principles in their musical and pedagogical conceptions."[6] Although he was initially successful, Hitler's rise to power in 1932 made all foreigners suspect, and he was separated again from teaching his students in Germany.

Through his writings, Dalcroze clarified his ideas and in 1920 he published *Le Rythme, la musique, et l'education,* a collection of essays written between 1898–1920. This book provides a comprehensive view of Dalcroze's assessment of the reforms needed in music education and the solutions offered through his method of teaching. *Eurhythmics, Art and Education,* is a collection of essays from the 1920s (published in 1930); in this book, Dalcroze discusses the effects of Eurhythmics on a wide range of subjects, including education for the blind, music and the cinema, and musical criticism.

At the end of his life, while trying to maintain the purity of his method, Dalcroze realized the deeply personal nature of the relationship between movement and music. His strength as an educator was not his ability to dictate the rules, rather it was his ability to observe the nature of musical behavior as revealed to him by his students.

The Dalcroze method has continued to spread throughout the world, and the amount of diversity within the method is everincreasing. The variability of the method is an affirmation of its strength. The rhythms of change in his method were, by their very nature, continuously progressing; Dalcroze would not have wanted it otherwise.

History of Eurhythmics

Any discussion of the Dalcroze method must begin with its evolutionary character. Since the method is based on the teacher's improvisation, it resists documentation. Improvisation is a personal expression and so the lesson depends on the teacher 's creativity.

Early on, Dalcroze observed that while his students were facile in their everyday movements, they were not so well coordinated when playing their musical instruments. He reasoned that if he improvised at the piano as his students walked to the beat, they would more deeply experience the music's rhythm. Then the students would transfer this feeling to their performance.

However, Dalcroze found the implementation of his philosophy was difficult because of his students' problems connecting their movements to the stimulus of musical sounds. The unsatisfactory messages between the body and mind inhibited their coordination. These difficulties were especially apparent when students began or ended movements too early or too late.

During these early experiments Dalcroze formed an important alliance with the Genevan child psychologist Eduoard Claparede. The main problem both he and Claparede intended to solve was how to improve and speed up the kinesthetic process. Because so much movement occurs on a subconscious level (we are not necessarily conscious of putting one foot in front of the other as we walk), students were not deeply aware of their movements to music. The breakthrough in Dalcroze and Claparede's study came when they experimented with exercises in excitation and inhibition.

While students moved to improvised music, Dalcroze spoke commands to alter their activity, forcing students to react with an appropriate physical response. At first the verbal cue "Hop" was used to indicate change. Gradually this was replaced by subtler musical cues as students exhibited greater and greater sensitivity to the musical improvisation. This became a spiraling process as Dalcroze continually demanded more attention to nuance. At the same time, he became increasingly aware of his students' limitations and his capacity to engender their Eurhythmic response. From this practice of stimulation/response/observation/revision comes one of the precepts of Eurhythmics instructors: The student becomes the teacher.

For the ancient Greeks, a strong influence on Dalcroze, both rationality and irrationality in music needed to be expressed in "eurhythmy" meaning good rhythm or good movement. The Greek idea of balancing opposites is central to Dalcroze's philosophy.

Eurhythmics is the study of contrasts: opposition in gesture, rhythm and meter, sound and silence, strict tempo and rubato. Dalcroze's process of Eurhythmics instruction progresses from teaching the "vibration of the whole body, to the nuance of isolated movements, to harmonizing them and then to opposing them, creating a bodily symphony."[7] He wanted each individual to understand how to balance these opposites and so to comprehend the nature of music and more deeply sense his or her own being. For Dalcroze, music affects the soul of the individual.

Dalcroze began his teaching explorations with several assumptions: first that music is fundamentally an aural experience and second that students begin learning music by listening. But these tenets were not enough to improve his students' performance. Problems occurred due to the undependable nature of rhythm and tempo and there was absence of musical power in student performances. Dalcroze concluded that "the mind perceived the variations (of time and rhythmic groupings) but ... was unable to give effect to them."[8] How could he reach his students' sense of rhythm?

Dalcroze's seminal realization about musical experience came from watching a person walk. Observing this ordinary occurrence he noticed that when we walk, we perform a regular pulse or beat—left, right, left, right. The speed or tempo of the walking may change—faster if we are excited, slower if we feel lazy, relaxed, or sad—but the regularity of the beat remains. Here was a new source of musical impulse to explore.

What secret lay in the ordinary experience of walking that held such promise for Dalcroze? It was the regular beat resulting from the body's attempt to balance itself—sensing weight, mass, gravity, speed, and inertia. When we take a step and swing the weight of our body onto one foot, our body is in a state of imbalance. It overcomes this disequilibrium by putting down the other foot. The body's forward motion demands that a leg moves in front to catch the torso before it falls. This action repeats on the other side. Because we have roughly the same physical weight on both sides of the body, the period of time required for this forward momentum for each side is almost the same. As a result, a regular pulse arises. The tempo of walking varies—but within a remarkably small range. If we go faster than a certain speed, we break into a run. At the other end of the spectrum, walking very slowly (try two seconds per step) is a challenge for most people. Few brides, coming down the aisle, can walk in time with the majestic wedding march from Lohengrin without some practice.

Although clapping in time with the beat is a common response to music, walking is a more vibrant expression of the beat. Walking forces us to move onward from one beat to the next—or fall down! The action of walking involves the whole body. We feel the movement in our knees, ankles, toes, elbows, head, shoulders, back, hips—all over. Walking uses balance as the principal force to propel the body ahead, supported by evenly timed leg movements. It provides a greater stimulation for memory impressions than clapping, which lacks the demands of balance and the impelling force of leg movement. Walking gave Dalcroze a simple, reliable source of stimulation for establishing in his students a sense of beat.

After he developed the idea of walking in response to music, Dalcroze experimented with establishing a beat using all kinds of movements including conducting, clapping, swaying, twisting, stretching, and skipping. He became keenly aware of the varying intensities of energy necessary to move specific parts of the body: a hand, a whole arm, a shoulder, or the entire upper torso. The body offers many ways of moving—each with a different flow of effort, direction, articulation, and speed. Dalcroze found the body to be an instrument in itself!

Different muscles can be used to mimic the different rhythms in music. Slow, heavy rhythms might be reflected by movements in the larger muscle groups such as the legs and torso. Quick, light rhythms might involve the fingers or the tip of the tongue. Dalcroze noticed that as students learned greater control over their large muscle groups, they felt a corresponding growth in control over the smaller muscle groups. These smaller muscle groups are vitally important for mastering instrumental technique.

Musicians, athletes, and dancers often "make it look so easy!" This apparent ease arises from repetitive practice—so that their bodies move smoothly and elegantly, without detectable effort, nervous obstructions, or mental and emotional distraction. With practice and training we can all gain some of this same ease and flow.

Head of Eurhythmics at the Longy School of Music in Cambridge, Massachusetts, Dalcroze instructor Lisa Parker tells of immense internal resources her students find while seeking to perform movements of greater effect and more sensitivity: "Once students start to use their whole body, it becomes like new words in a language. They find a richer vocabulary of behavior—'Oh, yes, I can use my body to understand this thing I didn't get, and this can speak to me.' They discover a lot of equipment in the back closet."

In other words, playing games with the natural forces of weight and gravity, and taking risks to find the limits of balance, enlarges a student's field of sensation and expression.

Dalcroze Students and Teachers

In preparing this book we interviewed Dalcroze students and teachers from different age groups, countries, professions, and skill levels to determine the effects of Dalcroze study on their daily modes of living. They responded with similar observations on many topics. Actor Abbott Chrisman describes his initial work with Eurhythmics:

> The work in [the Eurhythmics classes] made sense to me instantly. In a few days it was fairly clear to me what was going on. It was very exciting as it unfolded. What I have experienced since then is a progressive, continuing opening to the interaction of different components of the human system that has made for other kinds of growth. I think it's catalytic. I can't say that all the changes in my life over the last 10 years have been due to Eurhythmics, but I sure suspect that if this stuff hadn't happened, the changes might never have happened at all ... There's a different kind of concentration that comes along with this work—you have to be concentrated and open at the same time. You have to be ready for anything to happen, rather than the stock Western cultural definition of concentration: "Keep your eye on the ball." You know exactly where you're going to go. Before these ideas became real, I would solve problems head-on, tackling the difficulties. This other form of concentration, where you have to be absolutely concentrated and absolutely present, that's different.

Abbott went on to discuss his growing ability to rely on his own inner sense of the authenticity, the interrelated balance of what he was doing, both as an actor and as a teacher:

> I could look inside myself and find out whether something was working. This test was in me, instead of being outside. What Eurhythmics has done overall was make it possible for me to know internally whether or not something fit. What slowly came out of this was a set of internal sensations which was at first just physical but which began to grow and go beyond the physical. One of the things that was very powerful from the beginning was the sensation of a well-measured flow within the body, immediately authentic, trustworthy, and solid in a way that the intellectual experience with which I had been trying to run my life was not.

> I think there is a collective tendency to separate the sensory, mental, kinesthetic, emotional, intellectual, and spiritual aspects of experience. I say to my students, "You have these different ways of feeling but you have only one nervous system. All of this information is traveling along one set of railroad tracks to one railroad station."

Abbott's aim with himself and his students is to experience all the states of awareness at the same time. "It's only when we attempt to analyze and structure experience that we make these separations that are essentially artificial. That's the basic tool that Dalcroze taught me."

Several outstanding Dalcroze teachers recall their experiences in moving from a state of sensory imbalance that interfered with their musical development to a fuller experience of music and a more complete set of skills. Herbert Henke, Professor in the Choral Program and Eurhythmics at Oberlin College, entered his music studies aware that he was a strong visual learner. He felt however that he was "not very good at learning through my hearing. I had difficulty with dictation [listening to music and then writing the notes that represent it] and in memorizing. I could visualize the page and where the page turned, but if my [visual] memory failed me I was stuck! I had no other solution."

As an adult, he took an extensive course in Eurhythmics. He learned about Solfege, a technique that sharpens the ear through singing, and more about improvisation—creating music spontaneously. He observed that at first, "I hadn't the foggiest notion about what it would sound like when I improvised for quite a period of time." He eventually learned to play satisfactory improvisations. "This has been so exciting to me as an adult. I am so much better at hearing music and being able to use more than just my eyes."

Lisa Parker had the opposite experience. She could not easily translate the visual space of music on the page to a coherent musical rendition:

I could sight-read a single line, but I couldn't take a church hymn and put it into my hands. I just couldn't translate it. But if you sang it to me I could go right to the piano and know where it was. But the Dalcroze—that's what unlocked musical notation for me. I remember a sudden, light bulb experience when I realized a quarter note was a walking note. That seems simple, but it opened the whole thing. I said to myself, "Well, if that's what THAT is, then this is THIS,—and then THIS is—" and I was off and running! I knew how to commit to the written page. Somehow nobody had given me the physical experience as a child in piano playing; nobody had made that bridge for me. I don't know why, but it took the experience of the whole body to do it.

In Lisa's case, her musical ear, an aural system that conveys musical information to her brain, fingers, and voice, did not support a visual connection with music. It took stimulation of the whole body through movement to establish a sense of space on the page of music. She went on to say that "some connection got made neurologically for me—from visual to tactile—that happened because I started to use movement."

Plato stated "Education in music is most sovereign because more than anything else, rhythm and harmony find their way to the inmost soul and take the strongest hold upon it, bringing with them and imparting grace, if one is rightly trained, and otherwise the contrary."[9] Plato felt training people with the right music would produce good citizens to populate his Republic. Music's special property educated both the body and mind, not separately but together. Dalcroze also believed that music held a position of prime importance in education. He writes:

> The reason why I construct my entire system upon music is because music is a great psychic force, a resultant of our functions of mind and expression which, through its

power of stimulation and regularization, can bring order into all our vital functions ... music, more than all the other arts, is able to manifest in time all the various shades of our feelings.[10]

The use of the whole body in movement is at the center of Eurhythmics study. When Dalcroze realized that the swing of the body in a normal walk creates a natural pulse, he established the source from which all the rest of his work grew—developing not only a new way to learn about music, but a way to improve communication between body and mind.

At this point, we suggest you try some of the exercises on the compact disc (described in Chapter 8.) The heart of the Eurhythmics experience lies in actual participation; exploring some of the activities now will help clarify the information in later chapters. Once you do an exercise, be sure to write down your reactions immediately, while the impressions are still fresh. Subsequent repetitions of the exercises always differ from your first experience.

CHAPTER TWO

THE PROCESS OF
SENSORY EXPERIENCE

As living creatures we continue to exist because we successfully respond to our changing environments. We develop ingenious methods to gather, understand, and use information about our world. Once we receive information from our environment we assess it, make a decision about what to do, and take action. Each stage depends upon the previous: without information being received, there is nothing to assess; without assessment, decisions cannot be made; without decisions there is no action; without action there is no life.

This process of experience occurs over years or in a fraction of a second. Imagine standing next to someone striking a match. Our senses gather sensations and transfer them to the brain instantaneously undergoing the following steps:

1. *Sensory experience*: We hear the sound, see the glow, smell the sulfur, and feel the heat.

2. *Perception*: We blend all the relevant information into a single event.

3. *Attention*: We choose those perceptions on which we will concentrate.

4. *Memory*: We identify the occurrence and compare it to similar events in our memory.

5. *Action*: We assess the significance of the event and decide what behavior to take.

Because Eurhythmics classes are action-based, all the processes leading to action are important for us to consider. In later chapters we will discuss each of these steps and describe how Eurhythmics enhances each phase of the process.

Sensory Systems, Perception, and Memory

Our body's sensory systems receive information from our surroundings. The senses of sight, sound, smell, taste, and touch send messages to the brain. In addition, we have a sensory system that gathers information from inside our body, telling us about our physical position and movement. This is the proprioceptive system (proprio means 'one's own') located in special receptors in muscles and joints.

Sensory stimuli carry the individual strands of information such as bands of light wavelengths or speeds of sound vibration. The visual system mingles a pattern of light waves into a rounded shape or perhaps a shiny flat surface. The aural system blends a series of sound waves into a single message of deep resonant throbbing or clustered tinkling. Since both light waves and sound waves can emanate from the same object, such as a brass bell, sound and sight can be stimulated simultaneously. The more senses we stimulate, the more reliable our perception of the object.

As the collection of sensory information travels along the complex neural pathways, messages of little immediate importance are suppressed in favor of the available pertinent information. These messages form sensory units. We compare these for identification and meaning with previously stored memories. If there is a match between the present perception and a memory trace, we can identify the experience. For instance, the bands of light forming a rounded shape become a vase of flowers. According to our stored memories, we may consider the vase an object of beauty, a product of gardening labors, an object one must remember to water, or all the above.

A pattern in sound waves may match a memory of the opening chord of Beethoven's First Symphony. If the stimulus does not match any identifiable memory, the mind makes the best possible association using the most similar memory and establishes connections creating a new identity and meaning for this experience.

When stimuli stir our memory's network of associations, we theorize possible outcomes if we take this action, or that action, or perhaps no action at all. We may see a vase of flowers shifting its position and we feel intuitively this movement will cause it to develop a new relationship with gravity—in other words, fall over. Our brain checks where our body is, how far and in what position our body must move, sends messages to the appropriate muscles, and we rescue the vase.

The intuition that guides this movement arises from the sensory memories we began forming during our infancy. From our first breath, we begin our early experiments and explorations with objects and gradually build a bank of sensory impressions. An earlier event, such as a tower of blocks falling over, now prompts a remembered set of sensations, complete with eventualities: "When an object leans at such an angle, it will tumble to the ground."

There is another aspect of the falling vase included in the decision-making process: Is our instinctive action desirable? Is this vase of flowers worth spending the energy needed to save it? Is it a vase we never really liked and would be happy to be rid of?

Is the vase unbreakable, and the flowers a dry arrangement with no water to spill? If we move quickly will we risk pulling stitches from a recent surgery?

The brain assembles all this information, reaches a decision, and instructs the muscles to move or remain still. All this is done with lightening quickness. It is surprising that we do not more often misjudge the distance, the amount of energy needed, or the wisdom of taking action. All day long we make decisions based on information from the body's senses, calculations from the brain, and memory's emotional influence.

Sensory Experience from the Environment

Our senses keep us aware of the world around us and our place in it. Our sensory systems continually respond to stimulation from the environment, even gathering information while we sleep and are unaware of the outside world. In the sleeping state, millions of sensory synapses fire away for hours with all kinds of sensations, but none of this activity passes beyond the gate that protects our mind from sensory overload. For a time, sleep provides relief from reacting to incoming information. However, if the information load becomes heavy enough—the smell of smoke, crackling sounds, sensation of unexpected heat—our mind's sensory gate opens, arousing us to these sensations and the necessity to take action quickly! Self-preservation demands that our senses never stop taking in information; they do not rest. Only our conscious mind must have some "down time."

We can give our sense receptors a vacation by preventing stimuli in the environment from reaching them. If we cover our eyes we cannot see. If we stuff our ears with cotton we hear nothing. We instinctively hold our nose to avoid unpleasant odors. However we usually leave our senses available to the world to thrive on the information there.

Consider the contrast in sensory deprivation. This state is so foreign to our needs, expectations, and the very nature of our existence that for some it may cause psychological damage. Our minds and bodies are not prepared to tolerate this condition of emptiness. Many people, sitting in an anechoic chamber, isolated from the sounds of the surrounding area, report feelings of dizziness and discomfort. This deprivation makes us realize how much we need a vibrant sensory system to keep us healthy and balanced. We need to be aware in this world, which is so rich with sensation.

Sensory Experience from the People Around Us

External stimuli flow between the people around us and ourselves. We act both as a receiver and a source of stimuli for others. Being the receiver or the source of the message affects our perspective, but both ends of the communication bear certain responsibilities. The sender must ensure that the message goes out clearly and comprehensibly. The receiver must be attentive and ready to comprehend the message.

Because sensory signals travel along a physical path, the body's state can affect reception. It is the receiver's responsibility to keep a "reception center" ready for incoming information. This includes keeping the body that houses the sensory systems in good health, free from fatigue and emotional distraction, and well-exercised. A tired or disorganized receiver can defeat a lively, well organized, and sensitive sender.

Sensory Experience in the Eurhythmics Class

Musical messages come from two sources: the external environment (aural) and the internal environment (proprioception). The mind can blend and assess these two signals; however, we learn at an early age to attend to the aural signal while suppressing the musculature's impulse to move. Eurhythmics balances attention on both sources of stimulation and thus improves the processes of perception, attention, memory, and action.

Dalcroze's primary concern was his students' ability to hear. Although they were not literally putting their fingers in their ears, the effect was the same —they were missing information they needed as professional musicians. Dalcroze, as the information sender, had the initial responsibility to generate clear signals— musical tones performed with precision and musical flow. This duty he performed well. However, he had little control over the sound's reception. This was the students' responsibility. Dalcroze concluded his students were not listening with enough care or concentration and probably never learned exactly what to listen for. Thus, he focused on developing techniques to gain and hold the attention of his students. Attention is the final link in the successful transmission of any sensory communication.

All Dalcroze teachers must learn to send the clear signals that are so important to communication; sending is the only area where the teacher has total control. Once sent, the signal can be affected by the physical conditions it travels through (such as a noisy room) and the receiver's capacity to absorb the information. The teacher influences the signal's reception by catching the student's attention and by organizing the signal to contain features that please, intrigue, challenge, or soothe. The signal draws the receiver *into* the sensory message. This is the aim of Dalcroze teachers.

Dalcroze was especially successful in "packaging" musical information for sending clear and compelling messages. Descriptions of his classes show Dalcroze so in tune with his students that he could anticipate their response and so send them musical messages of great clarity and strength. One class description comes from Henrietta Rosenstrauch, an internationally respected Dalcroze teacher. While studying with Dalcroze she observed many of his classes. She remembers one class Dalcroze taught with a group of children from a poor section of Mainz, Germany:

> Inexperienced as these children were, and coming into a large room to be greeted by a strange man who did not even speak their language, they were understandably overwhelmed and clustered in the corners of the room. Dalcroze immediately went to the piano and started improvising music for walking and skipping. His improvisation was so irresistible that the children gradually began to move out into the room and respond to the music. When all were participating, Dalcroze suggested, through an interpreter, that they play a game of skipping to the music and then upon command, find a partner and skip together until another command when skipping alone was resumed. After several exchanges of partners, he then suggested that they clap simple rhythms with a partner. As the children experimented with these rhythmic patterns always accompanied by the musical improvisation of Dalcroze, their joy and enthusiasm grew—laughing as they would miss each other's hands when trying to clap the rhythms. To complete the demonstration Dalcroze invited the smallest girl in the class to sit on his lap and hold his arms tightly while he played. He then improvised freely, up and down the keyboard, crossing hands. The children were exhilarated. Any fear or dejection had completely disappeared. Instead, a happy group of children was exuberantly embracing one another after this one short experience with music and movement.

The Sender

Dalcroze teachers give commands to begin an activity or to change the activity mid-stream. Students, expecting a change command at any moment, focus their attention on listening. Therefore the teacher must time the commands so that the students can hear and respond without losing continuity. Once students gain a basic level of successful responses, it is important to scatter the change commands randomly so that students cannot predict when they will occur. While controlling the pace of expectation, the teacher continues to improvise without a loss of flow in the music. Accomplishing two simultaneous activities, especially in different modes of behavior (speaking and playing music), requires a high level of information processing within the teacher. Many Dalcroze students training for certification find this one of the most difficult functions to perform. "I can talk or I can play. I can't do both!" And yet, over and over, they learn to coordinate these two actions into a smooth whole. Learning to speak rhythmically, in time with the music, is one of the gambits that blends the two actions. Another is finding the most effective moment to speak, giving the students enough time to process the command and respond.

At the beginning of a Eurhythmics activity, the teacher cannot simply start to play or sing. Without a well-timed cue, the class will be late in joining with the first sound. Watch any conductor. They all command the attention of their musicians, lift their arms, and in the rhythmic pulse of the music about to begin, give a movement that precedes the first beat of the music. With such preparation all musicians begin together, and all students move as one. In the exercises in Chapter 8 and on the CD, we have provided such cues; as you listen to the CD, notice how these cues are timed to correspond to the music and the activity.

An informative incident recently occurred in a class composed of music specialists from various schools. After several weeks of Dalcroze classes, they had the opportunity to try teaching in this new mode. One class member, in her excitement to do well, presented a clear example of the unprepared beginning. She simply put her hands on the piano and began to play. The class lurched into activity. They caught up to her eventually, but did not experience the wonderful feeling of being "in concert." She recognized what had happened and at the next opportunity timed her preparatory words so well that the class moved off in perfect unison.

The Receiver

While the sender's elegance and clarity helps transmit a message, it is crucial for the receiver to be ready. Students should be listening (aural system), watching (visual system), sensing the surface of the floor (tactile system), and feeling the body position (proprioceptive system). They must be alert, listening for the slightest command, and standing in "ready position." Since many Eurhythmics activities begin with walking, "ready position" usually means standing with one foot slightly forward, carrying the body weight, and the back foot ready to swing ahead for the first step. This posture balances the body, induces a state of mental alertness, and prepares for the arriving sensations.

When the teacher is certain that her listeners are ready she catches their attention by saying "Listen" (or an equivalent command). She then plays a pulse on the piano or drum, claps, or moves for several beats, finally announcing "Go," or "Step," or "Walk." Class is underway.

Sending and receiving are both vital to good communication. Eurhythmics classes always include opportunities to listen carefully as a receiver and to send messages for others to follow. The teacher encourages even three- and four-year-olds to find their own ways to respond to music and then share their responses with each other. The children receive information through music and send information through movement, thus making a communication loop. When Janie's classmates are asked to try Janie's way of moving, they are receivers. Showing their response to Janie's movement they are senders. Janie communicates most effectively with her classmates when she moves in a well-defined, uncomplicated manner. Her classmates respond most effectively when they have watched and listened carefully, have internalized the feeling of her movement, and expressed it in their own.

Proprioception, the Sixth Sense

Proprioception, our sixth sense, conveys information to the brain about the body's position. Without looking, we know whether our arm is raised, our heel is off the floor, or our wrist is bent. Although we cannot see or hear our smile, we feel our smile because of special receptors in the muscles, tendons, and joints. The sensory messages from these receptors travel to the brain and influence any decision regarding action. How can we tell where to move—even whether or not we can move—if we do not know how our weight is distributed, where our bodies are in space, and how we are moving through space?

We are far more aware of information from our five external senses (vision, sound, touch, smell, and taste) than information from our sixth sense of internal or proprioceptive movement. Perhaps because so much of the external world is experienced through several modes at once—we see the dog, we hear the dog, we touch the dog, and we smell the dog—we are highly stimulated by the "dog." During our experience of the dog, we form proprioceptive memories about how far down we must reach to pet the dog—a memory so strong that we can recall the sensation without actually making the movement. We develop these move-ment memories, although we may not be very consciousness of them. As Margaret N. H'doubler astutely observed, "Movement is so basic a part of being alive that it is quite likely to be taken too much for granted. We fail to realize what a source of stimulating and satisfying experience it can and should be."[1]

While no less important than the five senses we learned as children, we often have to be reminded to pay attention to the proprioceptive sense. Were you ever surprised by hearing your mother, father, teacher, choir director tell you, "Stand up straight!" when you felt you already were? Other than a vague awareness that we are standing, sitting, or lying down, we tend to disregard information about the refinements of our body position and movement. We often tense muscles that have no effect on the action we are taking, like driving a car with the left ankle cocked to jump on the clutch or chewing our tongue when trying to remove a tight lid from a jar. If we increase our sensitivity to the information signals firing along our paths, we can easily eliminate these unnecessary actions.

Two kinds of specialized nerve receptors, kinesthetic and vestibular, inform the brain about pressure, energy, and ease of movement in such features as the tension in the muscles, the posi-tion of the limbs, and the angles of the joints. Kinesthetic recep-tors are located in the muscles, the tendons, and the joints; vestibular receptors are present in the ear. Like the other sensory systems, these receptors continuously fire impulses to the brain, keeping us aware of the shape of our body and our location in space.

The proprioceptive system is of primary importance in con-trolling body tension and relaxation. It feeds the brain informa-tion necessary for calculating how far, in what direction, and with how much energy the arms must move in order to send a basket-ball to the hoop. Such information is needed to balance time,

space, and energy—the three characteristics of movement famil-
iar to all dancers, actors, athletes and musicians. Only with rapid,
accurate calculations of these sensory movements can we produce
our imagined results. As athletes increase their proprioceptive awareness of time, space, and energy from inside their bodies and as musicians (athletes of the small muscles) recall more
and more accurately the sensation of moving a finger at a certain
angle, performance becomes more manageable, dependable, and
predictable.

Sensing Weight

In any action, the body constantly uses energy to counteract the
force of gravity. Music, too, "defies gravity" in a non-visible, non-
three-dimensional way. Such sensations include the music's rising
and falling, pausing and hurrying, and pushing and stretching so
that one long note seems to spin like a thread. We try to achieve
these musical sensations in the body.

When studying a piece of piano music, the authors have on
many occasions left the piano bench to sing and move to a phrase
in the music that was not sounding right, perhaps the fingering
technique seemed physically awkward. Feeling how the whole
body moved from one beat to another revealed subtleties in the
music that their fingers missed. "A bit of extra space is needed
between this note and that," or "The arrival on *this* note must have
more energy to keep it in line with the others," or "You've been
missing all the push in that phrase!" With a newfound awareness,
they return to the piano and find immediate improvement.
Practice is still necessary, but through movement, they discover
the sensation being sought.

A young student, Daniel, age eight, came to his lesson playing
a pattern of four equally long notes (dum-dum-dum-dum) with
the rhythm of "Happy Birthday" (dum-di-dum-dum). He had

practiced the pattern so thoroughly that he could not even imitate the correct way from my playing or singing. "Get to the sensation!" I said to myself, and I reminded him of his earlier experience of bouncing on the trampoline.[2] We both "bounced" our arms on the piano lid, recalling the sensation of the trampoline bounce through the whole body. Then Daniel played again, this time with perfect rhythm! His memory of the sensation successfully transferred to his arms and fingers on the piano keys, overcoming his incorrect habit. When the old "Happy Birthday" pattern occasionally crept in, all Daniel needed was a reminder of "Trampoline," and he was once again firm in his steady rhythm.

A teacher from Taipei, Fang-Chin Lin, relates a similar effect of simple walking in response to rhythm: "If I tell the children, 'Walk,' and they learn this from the beginning, then they enjoy all the moving. They enjoy it inside. After, when they come to the piano, the music is alive. The music is in their bodies. As they grow up they feel it more and more in their bodies—they feel the music and rhythm."

Sensing Space

The use of space is an important element in Eurhythmics classes. Teachers cajole their students into exploring space in individual pathways, rather than giving into the tendency to follow one another around the room like a herd of sheep. "Pretend your soles are covered with colored powder and you are leaving a trail of footprints—make an interesting design as you move."

Especially important for children are the ideas of sharing room space and respecting each other's individual space. Frances Aronoff, who could work wonders with small children, often had children establish their turf by drawing an imaginary bubble around themselves, pushing the ceiling as high up as possible and making the walls as far apart as they could reach. Then they drew a doorway and a doorknob, opened the door, stepped "outside," and were ready to move about. They now had their own place to come home to as soon as Fran called for this action during the class.

Often teachers simply remind students about rules of good classroom behavior that include respecting each other's space. Sometimes, a teacher may control the children's desire to push each other by challenging them to see "how close you can come *without touching!*" If such games are done musically, with movement tied to certain musical goals, the not-touching simply becomes the desired way to behave.

Developing Automatisms

Dalcroze teachers use the proprioceptive system to develop small habits of movement by which people learn to increase their physical control. During one of the conferences at the Jaques-Dalcroze Institute in Geneva, Reinhard Ring, present director of the International Federation of Dalcroze Teachers, gave a simple but distinctive pattern to move the body. He asked that we consider our feet to be the "bass" to whatever movements we made. He then directed us through a series of quick changes of rhythmic patterns for our arms, each a slight variation of the one before, while we moved around the room executing the bass pattern. To top this off, he added short phrases for us to sing in echo to his playing! Coordinating the voice and arms took so much attention that we could not possibly be successful without having first automatized the foot pattern. I was continuously surprised as I remembered to check what was going on below my waist. My feet were indeed faithfully performing the fast, little step of the bass pattern! While the concentration demanded in such exercises is immense, the experience of controlling complex actions builds self-confidence as well as motor coordination.

Why was automatism of any importance to Dalcroze? Music has many dimensions, all of them variable, over which a musician must exert control. Moreover, music is a composite of disparate parts moving in harmony. A barbershop or a string quartet must be aware of the melodic movements in all four parts, the volume level of all the performers, and the relationships in different simultaneous rhythms. For the body to integrate complex movements, the mind must cope and prioritize multiple messages. This applies to information of every sort, thereby providing advantages well beyond the realm of musical performance.

Proprioception in the Eurhythmics Class

Eurhythmics classes consider the body to be a musical instrument. It is treated with care and respect. Most teachers begin class with a warm-up that includes conscious breathing, gentle rotations of head, shoulders, wrists, and so on. Even with young children, the teacher begins with a gentle activity, such as walking at a moderate tempo, and brings about gradual escalation of the energy level. Sometimes a class will begin with a song in which the children echo "Hello." Then, one by one, each child is given a special kind of movement to make while the other children tap the pulse of the movement. Then all are ready to walk, jump, and run! Likewise, adult classes begin with small and simple movements like walking and hand clapping and gradually progress into more energetic and complex movements.

Beginning students learn to increase their sense of ever-present but often unnoticed information about their movements. This holds true for all ages. A direction as simple as assuming the "ready position" brings an immediate awareness of the disposition of the various parts of the body.

Additional activities encourage awareness of body parts we *can* move but do not (thereby losing flexibility) or that we move indirectly as a result of moving some other connected part (when did you last notice your elbows?) Adult students perform activities to foster appreciation for the wide range of movements which they can perform. Students become aware of such things as how elbows help move the arms with greater ease and power. Or, how by shifting the weight of a shoulder movement, we can turn quickly in a way that saves stress on the ankles and knees.

Humans are naturally flexible in the torso. Yet our surrounding environments are such efficient spatial arrangements that we seldom need to bend in our mid-sections. Ergonomic engineers strive to prevent large movements. We arrange frequently used items within arm's reach; as a result we exercise our arms a great deal at the expense of limiting other muscle groups. For those who work at computers, arm exercise is limited to nearly singular postures of finger movements. This habit of movement (or rather, lack thereof) has left us largely unaware of our torsos.

Eurhythmics teachers use torso games to fill their classes with images that evoke bending, leaning, and bowing. A teacher may say, "Reach out to paint the walls on either side of the room," or give instructions to "Move to another level." Such activities bring about grand movements. Working in pairs, one student holds a hand drum for their partner to tap, then shifts the drum to another location—and another and another. (The game comes in positioning the drum on accented or emphasized beats in the music—the partner must continuously stretch their torso to tap the drum on the unaccented beats.)

Small children can clap their hands (obvious and easy), then tap their knees, ankles, toes, shoulders, head, tummy, ears, mouth, eyelids, nose, and elbows. Then elbows touch knees, ears touch shoulders, toes touch elbows, and hips touch shoulders (impossible, but a funny movement that never fails to delight and arouse some flexibility in the torso). The objective of "torso games" is to increase flexibility through stretching and to increase awareness of the sensations of torso movements. The goal is to gain more control over these movements.

The aforementioned descriptions show how aware and responsive a Dalcroze teacher must be. What works with one class may not be successful with another. A "trick" used one day may not work on the next. Staying open to possibilities is crucial. A teacher must be alert to the moment when structured activities turn into mayhem and revisions (often quite small—a sudden change that calls attention back to the music) are needed. With music as the organizing force, Dalcroze teachers can let their students take risks and discover new experiences. The opportunity to experiment and explore in a physical way offers everyone, especially children, a fulfilling involvement of mind and body. It gives a sense of balance and releases the spirit of joy. This description of joy is repeatedly stated both by newcomers and people who have worked and taught for years. Eurhythmics invigorates, soothes, and satisfies.

Eurhythmics trains the whole body to respond to music, words, and even visual impressions. One of the most emotionally moving lessons I experienced as a student was observing children on a playground for twenty minutes without saying a word. After returning to the Dalcroze class, each student went to the piano and tried to give a musical depiction of one of their observations. Then the other class members attempted to name the activity. This exercise affected me profoundly because I realized that as I played the piano, I was re-experiencing my perception of such basic movements as swinging on a swing, lifting a toy shovel, and bouncing a ball. I was struck by the degree to which I take movement for granted and how rich with nuance, meaning, and emotion movement can be—if I consciously notice.

We often underestimate our capacity to get the message through our senses—we try to analyze an impression before we fully experience it. Dalcroze frequently complained about this aspect of rushing education. He deplored the school syllabus, in which music lessons caused children to attempt to "hear what they do not understand, read what they cannot understand, and write down what they have never learned or felt."[3] He believed the experience of the world must precede knowledge. He therefore developed ideas of music education along non-conventional lines: "I trained (my pupils) to react physically to the perception of musical rhythms."[4]

Information flows into our minds along two pathways: from inside our body (our proprioception that includes awareness of position, pressure, tension and relaxation) and from outside (our five senses of sight, smell, touch, taste, and sound). Simultaneous messages from external senses provides us a vital experience. The addition of enhanced body awareness through developing our proprioceptive sense helps us to embrace and better understand even ordinary events, like mowing the lawn or eating a meal.

In the larger picture of our lives, Eurhythmics can become much more than a method of music education—it is a consciousness raising process. This consciousness rests within our physical bodies in the form of bones, muscles, and nerves. Dalcroze realized the body is a vehicle, a source of sensations that fuels and guides expressive impulses. It is also a doorway from the physical realm into the imagination and spirit. As we communicate with others as well as within ourselves, the health of our body becomes of inestimable value to the health of society at large. As Dalcroze wrote:

> Is it not most important that we should feel perfectly balanced in ourselves, since life compels us to set up an equilibrium, both stable and flexible, between our individuality and society? Then let heart and mind, soul and body, live that same harmonious life which controls the muscular and nervous systems in the course of our physiological studies.[5]

CHAPTER THREE

PERCEPTION

Forming Perceptions

Perception is a process. Sensory stimuli move through the nervous system to the brain where they are analyzed and organized, thereby creating experiences in our consciousness. Perceptions form after the brain analyzes the sensory input. Seeing a vase, a person, or a burning bush begins with the visual sensations of brightness and shape. Our intelligence and experience completes the perception and we comprehend the known object. Sounds have meaning—a door slam, a high C note, or a snore—but only after they are analyzed. If we have never heard a sound before, it remains only a sound until we use other sensory input or knowledge to define it.

Perceptual Learning

Perceptions are learned, and much of this learning takes place at an early age. From the moment we take our first breath we are learning; there is even evidence that we learn in the womb. We experience sensations, develop associations between experiences, and eventually set up expectations. A set of brightness levels comes to mean a human face, the sounds accompanying the face arouse the comfortable feeling of receiving attention. A round object that changes its pressure against our hand becomes a rubber ball that can roll away from us, or be rolled toward us; the feel of its shape becomes "roundness." A wooden block becomes "square-ness." Out of these perceptions a basic intelligence develops that becomes the foundation for all cognitive learning.

Some theorists believe that the phenomenon of absolute pitch (being able to identify a musical pitch without reference to any instrument) develops in infancy. For children who are predisposed to this state (possibly due to heavy "wiring" in brain areas related to tonal memory) absolute pitch may develop when the environ-ment contains a sound source that frequently repeats the same tone, possibly the squeaky hinge on the bedroom door that always sounds just before Mother appears at the bedside. This is an instance of perceptual learning whereby a perception becomes deeply imbedded in the subconscious. Frank Lloyd Wright's biog-raphers make a connection between his early experiences with handling blocks of varied shapes and his mature sensitivity to shapes in his innovative architecture. These early perceptual expe-riences are established at such a primal level that in later years we are not conscious of having learned them.

Differences in Perception

Perceptions are influenced by the perceiver's state of mind as well as related information available at any particular moment. For example, if you are uneasy camping in the woods, you may inter-pret a small spot of light as the gleam in a wild animal's eye. A sea-soned camper may recognize it as a distant flashlight.

Consider the sound of human voices vibrating in harmony to the syllable "al." A choral musician might expect to hear the word "alleluia." A music theorist might identify a major triad. A listener with absolute pitch would recognize the key of B-flat major. A music historian would likely consider the period and composer, an acoustician the effects of the cathedral ceiling on the sound's resonance. A singer might sense the position of the tongue and throat as well as the pressure in the lungs and diaphragm. If the listener happened to be a singer with choral experience, as well as an acoustician, historian, and theorist, this single sensory moment would swirl with a myriad of viewpoints.

Just as a single event will produce as many perceptions as there are participants, an individual can experience many perceptions of a specific event. Each time we view the same picture, watch the same film, or hear the same recording, we actually have a new experience. Although the object is the same, our perspective will be altered. The second time feels different from the first time, the third from the second.

We describe these slightly different experiences as being the same. The differences, whether in the event or in ourselves, are so imperceptible that we are largely unaware of them. "I feel the same as yesterday," "I've heard the same thing from you before!" "I always sleep in the same position," "I make the same mistake every time." Realizing that we generalize our experience helps us understand how we compress our memory files—learning to identify approximations as the same.

Establishing a Prototype

As repetitions accumulate, we lose details of the individual experiences of "the same" event and blend them into a single memory impression, known as a prototype. The more often we experience a particular perception or sensory event, the more solid the prototype becomes in our memory. If the prototype is reliable, we can cope with an infinite variety of approximations without being confused about the true identity. Although each snowflake is unique, we have no trouble identifying snowflakes. Each child is unique, yet we easily differentiate "child" from lion or adult human. Moreover, when we limit our identification to one child, we learn to recognize that particular child wearing a red shirt or a blue one, with a suntan or without, with short hair or long hair, because the prototype of that child has become firmly imbedded in our memory. The prototype contains the critical, invariant features that make us certain of the child's identity.

Dalcroze teachers help their students from prototypes by seeing that every element of music is experienced in as many ways as possible. A steady beat is performed by walking, clapping, clapping someone else's hands, tapping oneself, tapping a drum, walking backwards, walking and clapping at the same time, walking in "Rockette" lines, doing all of the preceding in echo to another group, and so on. Once students experience so many versions of steady beat, they can trace the common element to a single identity. At this point, the perception of steady beat is reliably established as a well-defined prototype in the memory bank.

Applying Three Classic Principles of Perceptual Organization to Eurhythmics

The following three principles of perceptual organization are most often applied to visual images. We apply them here in order to clarify the way we organize aural perceptions, particularly music perceptions.

1. Figure and ground—focusing on the figure over the background.

2. Closure—supplying missing pieces in an incomplete impression.

3. Perceptual grouping—grouping by continuity, similarity, or closeness.

Figure and Ground

The Eurhythmics class described above focused on the perception of a steady beat. Steady beat is first perceived as the "figure" that stands out from the "ground" of the room, the people, and other stimuli in the environment. When the steady beat has become a reliable item in the class's movement repertoire, it can then become the ground for a new "figure," such as a melody or a rhythm. (Exercise 3 on the compact disc lets you experience this shift in attention from beat to a new "figure.")

Closure

The second principle—closure—is shown by our tendency to comprehend a complete object when some elements are missing. Consider how closure operates in vision: A drawing may show only the corners of a square, but we mentally extend the lines and "see" the full square. Does closure operate in our perception of steady beats? In any musical experience, once a steady beat is established, we tend to continue this sensation of beats internally—"hearing" them during any silent place in the flow of the music. (Exercises 5, 6, and 8 depend on closure—filling in the missing part.)

Perceptual Grouping

The three modes of perceptual grouping—continuity, similarity, and closeness—apply to various aspects of steady beat. Continuity is the essence of steady beats; it is the regular occurrence of a stimulus that sets up the expectation of recurring beats. Moreover, continuity suggests that beats will recur at the same predictable time interval. Similarity is a factor in perception if the beats are grouped by moments of silence, faster notes, slower notes, or rhythmic patterns of varied notes.

Closeness of beats also operates in our understanding of steady beat. Beat refers to the speed at which the music "walks"— the speed at which we might move in Eurhythmics class when we begin to feel the flow of the music. The aspect of closeness affects our bodily response and hence our sense of beat. (Exercise 9 lets you feel the difference between varying degrees of closeness.)

Enhancing Perception through Eurhythmics

Quoting the actor Abbott Chrisman again, we "develop a set of sensations that is at first just physical but then begins to grow beyond the physical."

"Beyond the physical" touches the heart of Dalcroze work. Accurate movement is certainly a desired outcome of careful listening. However, accuracy alone makes neither good music nor good communication. The body language so important to verbal communication also exists in music. For instance, students learn that clapping beats is not just moving the hands apart and back together in one position with one level of energy. Claps are essentially circular motions which vary in size according to how fast or slow the clapping tempo is. Claps can move in space from left to right "1-2-3-4" and back to the starting position again. This pattern of hand and arm movement arouses a feeling of flexibility and a flow through space which brings more than just accuracy to the musical phrase.

When Eurhythmics professor Herb Henke gives his exams, he guides his students into feeling flexibility and flow in their performances through the addition of movement:

> The students bring some music to class and play it. Then I ask
> them to play it again and select some phrase for movement.
> They move to the phrase, and we consider "How does it look,
> how could you change it." We play around with phrasing,

nuance, and dynamic feeling—I don't mean just loudness and softness, but a kind of vitality. I finally say "Now play it to match the way you are moving,." Sometimes the sounds they make are wonderfully improved and enriched. The students are excited because after being so conscious of technique and perfect performance, they regain this lost aspect of performing—they now can *feel* it again.

Henke describes a graduate student from Puerto Rico who said, "I never took an exam where I learned before!" She hugged him in her delight at having realized how her performance improved for those few phrases. "This kind of improvement happens over and over again," he adds. Students discover a world of different sounds in their playing and observe the tremendous value in the relationship between movement and hearing in music.

Henke's refers to a "kind of vitality" in describing the energizing effect that can come from intense awareness of the interaction of musical elements. Dalcroze teachers blend the aural perceptions of dynamics, beat, and pitches with muscular sensations of time, space, and energy. Out of this combination evolves a more subtle and expressive set of musical impulses and musical understanding.

The addition of body movement to music training increases the amount of sensory information forming musical perceptions. When the whole body is used, the nervous system draws information from many networks: not just the hands, but the arms, shoulders, rib cage, and hips. The eyes and ears, as well, join in a blending of sensory systems that reinforce each other in receiving and analyzing musical information.

The conscious appreciation of *how* we experience helps develop appreciation for *what* we experience. We can be conscious of an incoming flood of information before we think about or analyze it. We can enlarge the moment of perception—

concentrating awareness on the earliest split second, when sensations are strongest.

From our earliest years we learn to accept identification as an important process. "What's this?" we say to infants, hoping they can identify a ball, a hat, or a truck. But we also need to increase their sensory awareness—rub their hand over the surface, have them smell it, tap it, push it around, hold it. Using such sensory adjectives as soft, warm, shiny, sweet, and loud helps us hold an impression or sensation more effectively than do identifying nouns alone.

Verbal identification follows sensation and tends to reduce its effect in our memory. Eurhythmics focuses on the sensation itself, letting one moment develop into the next—seeking not identification but sensory continuity. Through Eurhythmics, people learn to use information fresh from sensation, before it has been consciously analyzed. One participant said, "I gained an understanding of music that music theory classes hadn't given me. It was on a more intuitive and feeling level combined with the intellectual—therefore deeper."

Inhibiting Perception: Adaptation, Competing Messages, Purposeful Inhibition

Psychologist William Hirst describes the process of focusing attention as establishing at least two levels of perceptions: those that are dropped into the background and those that receive focused attention.

Hirst states, "The organism selects among competing messages for at least two reasons: (1) because of limitations in its processing capacity and (2) because of the need to make sense out of the world."[1] The process of dropping information into the background happens through different mechanisms. Incoming information may be suppressed due to fatigue in the sensory systems, a chemical imbalance in the body, or because we purposely push information into the background position. Since taking action results from paying attention, thinking, and reaching a decision—we conclude that information that falls into the background is not acted upon. In general this is so, although inaction does not necessarily mean immobility. It simply indicates that there is no immediate decision to act.

Adaptation

> We know that the brain is especially sensitive to change, but relatively insensitive to steady state inputs.[2]

If sensations continue or repeat for a time, there is a kind of inhibition—a dropping into the background—that occurs. This experience is called adaptation. A steady-state sensory message causes a certain set of receptors and synapses to fire repeatedly for such a long time that their capacity to transmit signals is lowered and the signals no longer register within our conscious mind.

When the sensory system adapts to a steady-state message, the information it has been sending can disappear from our consciousness. This explains why you can look for a pencil you are certain was just in your hands, only to discover that you are holding it between your teeth. When the receptors in your jaw muscles reduce their firing rate to below the level needed to send the message, you become quite unaware of the jaw pressure holding the pencil. I even "lost" my youngest child one day when leaving a check-out counter at the supermarket. I looked around anxiously and discovered that she was in my left arm. I felt only an unspecified weight in my arm—it could well have been a bag of groceries. I had lost consciousness of shape and texture. Adaptation had reduced the sensations going to my mind.

Competing Messages

Imagine your morning commute. You are proceeding along your accustomed route and listening to the weather report on the radio. You are unaware of physical messages about your ankle, foot position, or even the sensation of a low-level headache. Your awareness is focused on the weather report, and your desire to head to the beach. You make sense out of your world by letting some of the available information recede from center stage, and paying attention to information judged more important.

However if another car (or bicyclist, pedestrian, or child) appears suddenly, your consciousness switches off the weather report and brings the sensations of driving to the forefront of concentration. In either of these states of consciousness—with the weather report or accident-avoidance at the center of your focus—you are maximizing and minimizing responses to various parts of the total information available. In both situations, competing messages are inhibited "for the good of the cause."

Purposeful Inhibition

Sometimes we must consciously choose to take in one message over another. Consider the cocktail party syndrome—too many voices pouring sounds into our ears, an orchestra in the background, doors opening and closing, silverware, plates and glasses clinking. We concentrate diligently on one person's voice, trying to follow the continuity of their words. To hear them better, we suppress much of the other talk floating about our ears. This is purposeful inhibition—the attempt to diminish the effect of one message in order to accentuate another.

We can exert inhibition consciously by substitution or diversion. People in the dentist's chair inhibit physical and emotional tension by listening to music, rehearsing poetry, or concentrating on relaxing their body. We all play games of distraction at certain times to focus the mind's attention on something more desirable than certain distressful sensory experiences.

To function well, we must suppress some competing messages. People who cannot do this have severe problems in making sense of their world. Children diagnosed with ADD (Attention Deficit Disorder) have serious difficulties focusing on specific tasks. They constantly absorb too much stimulation, and their attention flits from one locus of activity to another—continually distracted. These children find it difficult to learn because they cannot push irrelevant sensory impressions into the background and form well-defined perceptions in a cohesive manner.

Inhibition in Eurhythmics Class

Eurhythmics can help regulate the flow of information and focus perception. Over-excited children—those who always run when others walk, who bang into the wall rather than turn away in a gradual curve, who bang the drum instead of tap— can benefit from regular involvement in Eurhythmics classes. The very act of moving freely creates the opportunity to move in a different fashion. Contrasts are always important; if we can move with heavy feet, we can also move with light feet. If we can tap drums with a big stroke, we can also tap them with one finger. If we can jab and punch with accents, we can also bend and glide smoothly. I cannot count the times I have rejoiced at seeing a look of delight and self-satisfaction come over the face of a boisterous child who has just made the softest possible sound on a drum. What a delight! It is a wonderful accomplishment.

Eurhythmics is not a cure-all for discipline problems and anti-social behavior. However, when children learn a variety of behaviors with different energy levels, they learn they have choices. With music as the principal teaching tool, children can be guided into more acceptable social behavior. The attractiveness and immediacy of music captures children's attention in a way spoken words do not. When music gives the commands, they are likely to follow. The activity becomes a game. Being quiet and absolutely still is easier to do if stopping is part of a game. "Listen for it!" This is a way to ask for concentration on quietness that is rewarding because everyone can have the satisfaction of feeling "I did it!"

I must include a story about singing to my own children. When it was necessary to repeat the request that they put away their toys, I stifled the impulse to shout angrily by instead singing the words in a rhythmic way with a pleasant voice. (Oh, this did take self-control!) The result amazed me. The children looked up, decided this must be a game, and complied! Here was a new tool for my repertoire. It worked many other times—I think as much due to the effect it had on my own feelings as on the children's perception. The routines of the household became games.

I once described this technique during a session with general classroom teachers. The next day, one of the teachers came in with a story of her own. She had sung to her daughter, who was outside playing with friends, "It's supper time, time to come in!" In reply her daughter sang, in an equally pleasant voice, "No, Mother, not yet!"

Excitation and Inhibition

> While marching to music, the students are prepared to "... stop upon command and wait" for the predetermined number of beats before resuming the marching. This requires silent counting, great concentration, and a consciousness of the beat in the muscles as well as in the brain.[3]

We sense movement when something travels from one location to another, even when it travels through invisible space. We say music moves, and yet, where is it when it starts? Or ends?

Nevertheless, experiencing music arouses the effect of traveling from one location to another.

In general, we are aware of ourselves in moments of action but pay little attention during the interim periods of inaction. Dalcroze elevated inaction to an equal level of consciousness with action. He referred to the state of muscular activity as "excitation." Balanced with this was the state of "inhibition, "or moments when the musculature was inactive. Inhibition here meant purposeful control over the body's stillness, accomplished with care, accuracy, and lively feeling—a very positive state of inhibition.

In Eurhythmics class, inaction is not an absence of movement or a blank moment, but a moment of stillness filled with expectation and reflection. It is "active" inaction. Here motor control and emotional control work together to develop personal integration. When we are in a condition of movement, in an atmosphere of movement, in a space dedicated to movement, the urge is to move! It takes intense self-control to refrain from moving. Since we tend to become inattentive during inaction, it takes even greater control and concentration to hold the body in flexible poise and keep the mind alert while being still. Eurhythmics develops the capacity to move easily between excitation and inhibition and be in control at all times.

Controlling excitation and inhibition is important not only to musicians but to everyone—surgeons, factory workers, gas station attendants, hikers, and teachers. The ability to stop immediately at a warning shout, or even a slight gasp, could mean the difference between safety and danger. To shift easily and quickly between action and stillness, the body's networks must be aware and constantly assessing information—in control of the correct muscles, the correct amount of energy, and the correct sense of place.

At the first lesson, Dalcroze teachers (like driving instructors who first teach their students to stop the car) begin by giving their students moments to stop, wait, and then resume an activity. It is very important that stillness not be flabby or slack, nor should it be tense with expectation. To this end, Dalcroze teachers watch their students' posture during moments of silence. Are their knees straight and locked or slightly bent and flexible? Have their shoulders sagged and their backs curved? Are they leaning slightly forward, with a look of readiness to go ahead or turn quickly to go in another direction? Do their eyes express a state of listening? If students have slumped during a pause or have a rigid stance, they are reminded of the need to be alert and ready to shift on a moment's notice.

Teachers vary the length of the pause between phrases of movement so that the return to movement is unpredictable. Sometimes they change the relationship between music and movement—students stand still and listen while the music plays and move when the music stops. In working with others, whether in pairs or in a circle, students tap on some beats and are still on others according to the commands of the music or the teacher's voice. We echo Ecclesiastes, "There is a time to play and a time to be silent," but all the time must be filled with listening.

CHAPTER FOUR

ATTENTION

There is an old story about the farmer who bragged that his wonderful mule understood everything he said. When asked to demonstrate this amazing feat, the farmer picked up a two-by-four and gave the mule whack on the head. He explained his technique saying, "First, I have to get his attention." Dalcroze used much gentler means, but he, too, understood that first he had to get his students' attention.

Attention serves as the bridge between perception and memory. Stimuli may travel through the sensory system but not be perceived; events may be perceived but not remembered. Although much of what occurs within our personal world falls by the wayside, our memories store vast quantities of impressions at various levels of retrievability. Some impressions are stored in a manner that makes them easy to retrieve; some are faint and hard to recall. The primary factor in determining the level of retrievability is the level of attention operating during perception.

Attention as a Skill

Theories of selective attention and divided attention express the idea that attention is a resource of limited capacity.

Proponents of the theory of divided attention submit that even if we could do several things at once, we would perform each task less well than if we undertook them separately. Performing several tasks simultaneously limits our processing resources, resulting in stress on our systems and reduced performance.

Psychologist William Hirst explains that processing requires resources to function smoothly: "If we assume that there is only a fixed quantity of resources, then the difficulty in doing two things at once occurs because there are not enough resources to 'run' the processing adequately."[1] Experiments where subjects were required to complete several tasks at once show evidence that it is easier to perform multiple tasks if different modalities are involved, such as listening to one thing while viewing a second different element. Additional experiments conclude that subjects can more easily deal with a second task if the first task is made automatic. However, Hirst explains, "Scientists are still unsure about the resources for doing more than one task at the same time…Indeed, almost nothing is known about the difference between automatic and effortful processing."[2]

Hirst conducted a study that offered a different conclusion about one's capacity for paying attention. In this experiment the subjects were directed to read and write at the same time. Neither of these activities could be done automatically. At first the subjects balked, feeling they could not possibly pay simultaneous attention to two such demanding activities. Six weeks later they performed both tasks equally well—with disbelief that they were upset in the beginning. They even expressed amazement that they could have initially considered the task impossible. Hirst came to a conclusion that has particular significance for Dalcroze teachers:

> The limits [on attention capacity] can change with practice and depend on individual abilities. At any particular stage of

development, a limit exists as to what a person can or cannot do, but additional practice can change this limit.[3]

Hirst's experiment demonstrate that attention is a learned skill, not a limited resource. Dalcroze teachers employ this idea when they push the limits of their students' attention, widening their scope and increasing their sensitivity.

Developing Attention through Eurhythmics Games

As Dalcroze worked on his early experiments in improving music training, he relied on the advice and collaboration of psychologist Eduord Claparède. Claparède developed a hypothesis that teachers could not teach properly unless they had their students' attention. Following this line, Dalcroze and Claparède devised musical games to focus students' attention and to improve their attention through training.

Dalcroze developed the skill of attention by having students move their entire bodies to music—through space, in time, and with energy. Through the direct and total involvement of their bodies, Dalcroze could guide their senses and influence their perceptions as they formed the habit of focused attention.

Dalcroze understood that attention must remain at a high level throughout an exercise and throughout the whole class. He saw how quickly students became habituated to a sound or a movement—their bodies moved, but their minds were disconnected. Dalcroze used all his improvisational skills to introduce small changes; each change in the music required a change in movement. It might simply be a shift from walking forward to walking backward, stopping promptly at a verbal or musical cue, changing from walking to clapping, or walking to tip-toeing. What mattered most was the fact of the change not the content. "Any break with expectancy is the trigger for attention and learning processes."[4]

Eurhythmics Games

Eurhythmics games can work in many situations—from classrooms to therapy sessions. They are more like guidelines than specific activities. Teachers use them, as Dalcroze did, to devise activities suitable to their class's current need. The games describe a process for raising the attention level but do not dictate the content. They are totally adaptable to a wide variety of classes with multiple levels of accomplishment, to musical materials from far-flung sources, and to different age groups with broad ranges of physical skills.

The essence of the games is to arouse and focus attention, for the enriched experience of the moment and for clear, easily retrievable memories. Their value arises from an understanding of human behavior.

Follow

As he trained students in focusing their attention, Dalcroze instructed them simply to follow the flow of his music and to express with their bodies the beat and quality of sound (loud or soft, connected or separated, increasing or decreasing in volume). With his musical improvisation at the piano, Dalcroze followed one change with another, constantly breaking the stream of expectation. This device works for all ages and levels of sophistication.

Beginners may be challenged to respond only to the tempo of the music, walking faster or slower as the music changes. Once the teacher sees that the students are responding smoothly, it is time to add another change—perhaps a shift in volume. The students may respond by changing the way they place their feet on the floor. The teacher may increase the tempo and play very staccato sounds to stir the feeling of jumping, or decrease the tempo to very soft sounds for tip-toe walking. An intense bond develops between the teacher, the music, and the students. The teacher totally concentrates on the activities of the students, always gauging their readiness for the next step. The students listen intently for the next shift in the character of the music, trusting that the music will tell them what to do.

In more advanced classes, students may begin by simply walking to the pulses of the music. The teacher may then play an accent, say, on every fourth pulse (a new sound) to which the students respond with a knee bend, a shoulder lift, or an arm movement—something that says to the teacher, "Yes, I hear what you are doing." The teacher may give a specific instruction such as: "Walk the pulse, and let your claps follow any changes you hear in the accents." The teacher changes from groups of four to groups of five for a while, then to groups of another size. Throughout the activities she changes tempo, dynamics, and articulation (connected—legato, or separated—staccato). Working on such multiple elements sends the attention levels soaring! Teachers try to keep their students balanced between feeling comfortable and feeling a bit at risk. The students learn to follow all changes quickly and smoothly. (Exercises 5 and 7 in Chapter 8 and on the CD are examples of "follow" activities.)

Quick Reaction

Quick reaction games specifically target the problems most people share with Dalcroze's students: rushing an activity or hesitating too long for an action. The students learn to respond quickly and with balance and control to the musical changes. The teacher often arranges musical or verbal cues (a quick high note on the piano, a drum sound or a wood block, or the word "change" or "hup") to alert the students to the change immediately before it occurs. The students then have a given amount of time to respond appropriately, usually by the next beat. The teacher's commands must be times so exactly that the whole class makes the change at the same moment—smoothly, appropriately, and without tenseness of abruptness.

A quick reaction game can be as simple as changing the part of the body used for tapping the beat. With a beginning class, the teacher might mention a tapping location, the command being "Head," later "Knees," later "Elbows," and so on. Eventually, the command for specific body parts is replaced by the word "Change" thereby encouraging the student's creativity in selecting the area they choose to tap.

Students in Dalcroze Solfege classes are given quick reaction challenges to keep their attention focused while singing. The process of coordination developed by moving the large limbs of the body functions also in controlling the small, even minute, movements of the vocal folds, diaphragm, and lungs. On command, students repeat whatever note they are singing until a second command tells them to proceed with the melody. This small trick gives the teacher an opportunity to stress a critical note by calling for repetition, and keeps the students focused on the activity. Other commands are to sustain a note for an extra beat before proceeding to the next note, or to skip the next note at command and pick up the melody two notes further on. Such challenges coordinate listening and concentration while developing performance control. (Exercises 3, 4, 8, and 13 stress quick reaction activities.)

Dalcroze designed a more challenging quick reaction study using a process known as disordination. As soon as a physical and musical idea had been grasped and brought under control by the students, Dalcroze worked to disorient or disordinate them. Rubbing the tummy and patting the head is a kind of disorienting exercise. Dalcroze combined asymmetrical movements that called for different motor commands at the same time. He had students begin by conducting two-meter with one arm, then at a command, adding three-meter for the other arm, and at a later command adding a knee dip on every fifth step! The exercise was not intended to perfect the physical combination of movements, rather it was meant to practice expanding a high level of attention into various parts of the body. Students learn to coordinate the movements and pay attention to their quality. Learning to control such demanding kinesthetic experiences prepares the body and mind to skillfully manage movement in other difficult situations. This develops close communication between sensory messages, the mind's decisions, and muscle responses.

Replacement

Another variation of quick response games, replacement games, begin with a simple matrix, such as a grouping of six steady beats. These can be walked, tapped, or sung. The teacher watches to see when the students are comfortable and mindful of the beat group length. Perhaps they turn toward a new direction at the beginning of each new beat group to communicate their awareness and to assure the teacher that they understand. Then the teacher calls "Six," which means, "Replace the sixth beat with a rest." (Students do not take a step on "six.") When this is going well, he calls "Five" and so on. Each time the students rest on the called beat, replacing movement with stillness, sound with silence. Another form of the game is to vary the time between changes and the order in which the numbers are called. This game requires concentration, alertness, and motor control.

There are many variations. Sometimes a pattern is established: "Perform the replacement on '6' four times and then move on to '5' four times, and so on." In this case, the teacher gives no instruction. The students carry the full burden of remembering the order, where they are in the series, and how many repetitions they have done—as well as continuing to move smoothly and with a musical flow.

Replacement can be done by substituting a selected pattern for each beat in turn:

dum-dum-dum-dum
diddy-dum-dum-dum
dum-diddy-dum-dum
dum-dum-diddy-dum
and so on.

In Exercise 11 (in Chapter 8 and on the CD) the activity selected to replace each beat is a change in body position; another example of replacement can be found in Exercise 8.

Canon

A different type of exercise is based on the musical device known as canon. In a canon there are at least two parts: the first part initiates and the second imitates. There are two types of canon, interrupted (echo) and true.

Interrupted Canon

Interrupted or echo canon is the easier of the two types of canon. In echo canon, the leader makes a musical statement and then rests while the follower performs the imitation. The follower then rests and listens while the leader performs the second phrase. It's like call and response singing in folk music, where the leader sings and the group echoes.

In Dalcroze classes we perform rhythm canon with hand claps or drum taps, with movements, with words, or with the piano. (It could be done with any instrument.) I have done this in piano lessons by sitting in the middle of the piano bench with a child on either side. Sometimes both children echo what I play. Other times while I am playing, I call out which child is to echo next. This game requires close attention, good short-term memory, and quick motor response. Sometimes one of the children becomes leader and improvises the music. (Exercise 14 is an interrupted canon.)

True Canon

The true canon is more difficult than the echo canon. It is more accurately a round, such as the child's song *Row, Row, Row Your Boat.* In Dalcroze classes, however, the music is improvised by the leader. The follower has no idea what the musical pattern will be and must listen with great attention to reproduce it accurately. When the leader continues without interruption into the second part of the activity, the follower imitates the first part and *at the same time* listens to the leader's second part. This device stretches attention and internal memory. True canon is an advanced exercise. (Follow Exercise 15 to understand a true canon.)

The five games just discussed make different demands on the mind. The Follow is reactive—students must pay attention to the stimulus, respond quickly with a suitable match, and be sensitive to all details of the music. In the Quick Reaction exercise, students must attend carefully and remember to listen for the cue and make the changes. Replacement requires greater involvement of the mind; the student must remember a pattern of manipulation and apply it while in motion. The Interrupted Canon demands retention of a specific musical phrase for a long enough time period to guide the response. True Canon makes the same requirement and adds the necessity to listen to new stimuli while performing the previous part.

Within each category there are multiple levels of challenge. A Follow can simply include a change in tempo, or it can incorporate several movements such as performing one rhythm in the arms, another in the feet, and showing accents with the head in response to different, simultaneous musical patterns. It is like preparing lunch boxes, pushing a cupboard door shut with a knee, and talking on the phone—all in time to the music!

Techniques for Arousing Attention through Eurhythmics Games

In devising these successful games, Claparède, with his knowledge of human behavior, and Dalcroze, with his keen observations, utilized techniques similar to those used by psychologists for arousing and sustaining attention—sudden change, contrast and novelty, intensity, repetition, complexity, and motivation.

Sudden Change

Quick reaction games involve two or more contrasting activities. After introducing two activities to the class, the teacher establishes an aural cue—either verbal such as "hup" or "change," or musical such as a high note or a distinctive chord. The cue tells the students to change from one activity to another. Quick reaction activities combine such contrasting actions as walking forward and backward; bouncing a ball on the floor and tossing a ball in the air. There are infinite possibilities. The important characteristic is the *unpredictability* of the moment of change. The uncertainty keeps attention focused on the activity—it must be a *sudden* change. (You can try a quick reaction exercise by doing Exercise 4 in Chapter 8 and on the CD.)

Contrast and Novelty

All quick reaction games are based on the contrast of at least two different activities. Contrast and novelty are characteristic of many Dalcroze activities. As an example of contrast, consider ball-passing games performed in a circle where excitement is created by passing to the left and then to the right. Novelty arises when students have varying periods of time in which to pass the ball (one beat, five beats, whatever the teacher chooses). As the time period lengthens, each student must keep the ball moving by putting his arm up, around, in a figure eight, or in any other fashion that is new and different from the others.

Try "Twice as Fast and Twice as Slow" (Exercise 9 in Chapter 8). This begins as a quick reaction game, with specific commands to promptly respond. Part way through, the instructions say "The music will tell you." At that point, the flow of the music itself feeds the messages about how to move. The critical feature throughout is the contrast between the two types of steps.

Intensity

Another aspect to getting students' attention is intensity, or the energy level of the stimuli. Rising energy levels can occur in any Eurhythmics game. We can increase intensity by a gradual change from soft to loud while clapping or tapping a drum or sounding our feet on the floor. We can see intensity in such movement as arm swings that begin small and close to the body and then move farther and farther up and out thereby using more and more energy. Students can physically feel it when they face each other, press palms against each others' palms, and increase or decrease the amount of pressure between the palms.

Drawer Pull (Exercise 6) draws attention to muscular intensity. Laban Effort Actions (Exercise 2) illustrate the various levels of intensity. In Flick and Glide (Exercise 10), two of the intensity levels combine in simultaneous movements, showing both intensity and complexity as means of arousing attention.

Repetition

Repetition is a powerful tool that can be used to attract students' attention. Activities usually develop by changing our movements; the repetition of a single pattern is a stark contrast, which in itself arouses attention. The repetition of a single pattern conveys that something needs to be listened to more carefully. Students may be missing a detail the teacher feels they should hear. I use this device often when I notice that students are observing only the durations of the rhythm pattern and not its quality (louder or softer, separated or smooth). I repeat the pattern I have just played, I play it again, and then another time. The students give me inquiring looks, wondering why I am doing this. They then smile as they realize my message is, "You are not listening with full attention!" This approach is a wonderfully effective non-aggressive way to alert students that they are not performing up to their potential.

Repetition serves another purpose in exercises such as the Drawer Pull (Exercise 6). The same movement is repeated numerous times to instill a deep memory of that movement's sensation. These internalized memories can later be recalled for use with one's imagination for internal planning and guidance.

The design of Echo Canon (Exercise 14) is based on repetition. In this activity, the leader states a musical pattern and waits for its repetition by the others. The repetition itself, translated from an aural activity to a muscular one, makes a more memorable impression of the pattern.

Complexity

Increasing the complexity of an exercise by using diverse elements forces an increase in attention. Flick and Glide (Exercise 10) is a complex exercise that combines two levels of intensity, walking one pattern and clapping another. In True Canon (Exercise 15) the level of complexity is raised considerably, with continuous contrast and change. For this you must move to what you have just heard and at the same time listen to new material you must subsequently perform. Notice your level of attention! (Remember to write your observations about your performance and your personal responses immediately after performing the exercise.)

Motivation

All Eurhythmics exercises encourage motivation because of their game-like quality. The challenge of executing a task slightly above your ability to perform well builds confidence. The teacher's observations and skill in judging the level of the challenge is critical to the success of the students. Too little challenge results in boredom; too much produces frustration. When the games contain opportunities for challenge, success, experimentation, and sharing, the desire to improve runs high. When this emotional state exists, there is heightened sensitivity to everything that is experienced.

The innate pleasure and satisfaction of moving freely to music is in itself a great motivator. Dalcroze was a great tease, full of jests and surprises that filled his classes with the air of a joyful playground gathering. Beatrice Hodel, who taught at the New York School, describes a similar play-like atmosphere: "It's just second nature to me, sitting on the floor with the children. I remember distinctly when Miss Nina (from the school's business office) would come to the door—and I'd roll the ball to her! It's just play. You have to be on the same level as the children. You can't be an authoritarian."

❧ ❧ ❧

Are you standing tall? Are your hands clenched? Toes curled? Does your arm hang heavily in complete relaxation or is there some tension in your elbow or shoulder? As we gain information about our body's position and movement, we gain control over and appreciation of our actions. Frequent, brief moments of attention to signals from our muscles and joints can increase our awareness of this flow of information and can help develop keener memories of sensations.

Using our bodies with greater ease, balance, and beauty is a worthy goal. Using our minds with concentration, focus, and alertness opens possibilities we might have otherwise missed. To accomplish this through the impulses of music creates experiences of renewed joy and delight. This expression of attentiveness is what Dalcroze strove to develop through his demanding games, understanding that the inattentive child is likely the unchallenged child.

CHAPTER FIVE

MEMORY AND ACTION

The preliminary determiner of whether an event or concept will be remembered seems to be the type of processing given to it at the time it is experienced. If the information was integrated into a schemata or action, it is likely to be remembered. Otherwise it is not.[1]

The Memory Process

Memory involves the encoding of incoming information for storage and its subsequent retrieval. The retrieval of memories is essential for recognizing new information and preparing it for storage. Experiences create memories; memories help modify and recognize experiences. We are not born with a bank of memories; we learn all our perceptions, we form our memories.

You will recall (as you retrieve from your memory!) that learning begins in infancy. At this time the "storage bins" of memory begin filling. The infant's world is full of diverse sensory experiences. These sensations, including a growing awareness of cause and effect, build the memories each child relies on to make sense of the world. As memory banks grow larger, more vibrant, and more interconnected, more events in the world start making sense.

Whether or not we understand our perceptions depends on how well the incoming information fits with previously stored data: "Is this a sound I have heard before? Is this a fresh smell? Is the toast burning?" If the incoming information is new—not renewed—it will have no corresponding description in our memory banks. We accept the unfamiliar sensation as unrecognizable, unidentifiable, and possibly dangerous!

Perhaps the incoming information stirs a faint impression. Maybe we experienced it before, but did not pay close attention, and therefore did not store it as a vivid impression. So the information may be recognized but not identified. In this condition, memory has little value in determining action. However, when the incoming information finds an accurate match, identity is certain and all the near and distant connections are stimulated. The mind can then quickly assess the situation and determine how to respond appropriately. Such thinking depends upon the successful storage of vast amounts of readily retrievable memories.

While certain locations in the brain have specific control of the ability to recall information, memory involves many areas of the brain. The ability to learn and recall is a process that involves three functions: 1) encoding information from sensory and motor structures, 2) correlating the encoded material with arousal or motivational states, and 3) retrieving information for working out a goal, appropriate strategies, evaluations, or corrections.[2] A breakdown in any of these functions impairs the memory process.

Encoding Information

Encoding an experience is the first step in the formation of memories. Encoding is most successful when elaborate connections are established with existing memories. If there are few available associations, as when you begin to study a new discipline, then your memory traces will be shallow and difficult to retrieve. As you accumulate more knowledge and experience, an ever-tighter network of connections forms. This is why Eurhythmics is such an effective way to learn. The encoding of a single moment involves a heavy load of connections including motor messages from all over the body as well as aural, visual, and tactile sensations.

Sometimes we encode an experience in a superficial way because we accept it without paying attention to its connections; we allow some of the stimulation to drop into the background. Without the enrichment of our attention, the memory soon fades. Have you browsed through a magazine in the doctor's waiting room and not been able to recall a single item you looked at? If we glean the meaning of the written word, have an image of what the word represents, and relate it to the categories to which it belongs—people, places, smells, foods, and so on—the memory is likely to survive. In his recently published book, *Searching for Memory,* Daniel Schacter calls this process elaborative encoding, in which we "*reflect* on the information and *relate* it to things we already know."[3]

Psychologists emphasize the importance of structure, saying that memory storage cannot be a random collection of thought. Efficient storage demands that interrelated information be highly organized. Music is a highly structured event; it provides a succession of patterns that build a structure of continuity and integrity. Moreover, music uses systems of highly integrated relationships. The performance of music challenges the validity of its structure, testing it, reshaping it, and strengthening it. Music's structure may facilitate smoother processing along the specific pathways of brain functions. People with certain brain lesions, who are incapable of talking, can produce words when they sing. Processing words through music apparently provides a viable structure that they have lost in another area, a way of ordering and regulating the flow of neural impulses that form words.

Arousal and Motivational States

The emotional and motivational parts of the brain known as the limbic system existed well before the development of the neocortex, the thinking parts of the brain. Part of the subcortical structures, the limbic system was imperative for survival at a time when the world demanded immediate action without the luxury of time for decision making.

Humans have not lost their swift limbic response. I witnessed just such a response one day when my husband and I were hiking in the Snowbird mountains of North Carolina. We were coming down a wide footpath near a clear, bubbling stream. My husband, who is usually in good control of his emotions, physically alert, and self-confident, suddenly jumped more than twelve inches off the ground. He glanced to the side of the path and saw a snake stretched out on a large rock, warming itself in the sunshine. My husband is not afraid of snakes. (This snake was smallish and certainly harmless.) Yet at the moment of his perception, his body was propelled into explosive action triggered by a primitive response, from a level well below the thinking frontal lobes. Moreover, the experience was fraught with a high level of emotion, cementing it as a vibrant and long-lasting memory for both of us—I with my perspective and he with his.

Scientist Hans Markowitsch demonstrates the interdependence between emotion and memory by showing that memories are remembered best if their content is highly emotional.[4] Research indicates that particularly well-remembered events, whether involving sensory, perceptual, or reflective abilities, are linked to emotion. Material in short-term memory passes into long-term storage only if there is sufficient emotional significance tied to that event.[5] Delacour, a leading cognitive psychologist, suggests that the best way to improve skills and memory in mentally handicapped and impaired individuals is through arousal, motivation, and stimulation.[6]

Arousal, or sensory excitement, is an important part of Eurhythmics. Dalcroze student Abbott Chrisman observed: "When you do these exercises and do them right, there's a sense of well-being, a sense of feeling good." This state of feeling good, with our senses aroused, helps us form strong memories about the musical elements and the movement sensations we experience in these classes.

Sometimes we are the victims of unfortunate experiences forced upon us by outside circumstances, such as witnessing a car accident or standing near a tree at the moment of a lightning strike. Any such event commands attention at a heightened emotional level. The memory remains brilliant and clear, readily retrievable for life. Our voluntary experiences can also be consciously noticed, in detail, and with heightened emotion. Did you ever lie in the grass and stroke a single blade, noticing its texture and temperature, feeling how tightly it was held in the sheath where it came out of the ground? Have you noticed with care the effect of light on newly washed hair, or compared the fragrance of oregano to marjoram? In any of these examples, the intensity of sensory arousal assures storage of a vivid memory that can be reviewed in the imagination at will. Events become part of a "reference library" that identifies similar future events or related connections.

Retrieval of Information

Storage exists for the purpose of retrieval; we constantly compare now with then. Thus the chain of memory grows—stimulus, perception, storage, and retrieval. The success of retrieval relies on the strength of the sensory impression, and perhaps to a greater extent, on the elaborateness of the connections. We must be able to "see" an item clearly in our mind's eye in order to find it again. If we place an object such as a car key in a bright box, put it near other things related to its use, and tell someone in detail where we put it, then we are likely to quite successfully retrieve the object. If we repeat this ritual the next day and the next, the memory of the process of retrieval itself helps us find it. Every re-use of this memory establishes more connections. We will have the memory readily available even in moments of stress. Just such a result is expected of firemen, ambulance workers, stage performers— anyone who must be able to recall information immediately and respond under pressure.

Our mind races through our "reference library," finding a match between incoming information and previously stored associations well endowed with connections. It brings forth the "match" to working memory. From there our minds can proceed to the next step of either storing the incoming information, mingled now with its match, or using the information for immediate action.

When stored impressions are retrieved from long-term memory and brought into working memory we can work towards goals, strategies, evaluations, and corrections. In this stage of working memory we can make decisions about possible actions. Making the actual decision may not require much time, as when, for example, a Dalcroze teacher calls "Go" or "Change" and expects students to respond immediately. However, consider how many memory traces must be alerted for the body to engage in this behavior. Several senses were activated, perceptions were formed, and information was identified and then coordinated into messages. These messages were sent back to the muscles telling them how to change their position. All of this happens in a split second. Other types of behavior require considerably more time for contemplation, such as writing a book, discussing a policy, reviewing a plan, or performing a complex mathematical calculation. This sort of decision-making involves retrieving many images, trying out new relationships, manipulating information—tossing, transposing, reshaping—until our intuitive sense of what should happen is satisfied or exhausted!

Learning and Memory Systems

If you consider that every event is "the first time," then every experience becomes an opportunity for learning. Learning requires memory. There is a brain condition that causes some people to lose the capability to remember present day events; in order to have any continuity, these people must write down everything they hear, see, and do. Although they retain memories from the time period before this brain malady developed (even complex technical knowledge), they cannot learn anything new. There is no memory for incoming events.

Sometimes we ardently wish we could delete the memory of something foolish we have just said or done; we wish we could erase the sensation of something unpleasant we have touched or smelled. Unfortunately, these uncomfortable moments are very likely the ones we will remember with the most pristine clarity because of the intense emotional content. Given the choice of losing these moments or retaining the capacity to remember, we would surely opt for the latter.

The following sections discuss several systems of learning and memory which are enhanced by Eurhythmics classes: Sensation and Imagery, Multimodal Memory, Muscle Memory, and Internalized Sensations.

Sensation and Imagery

From an early age we experience sounds that gradually change character, from loud to soft to fast to slow to high to low to long to short. Like the movement of our body, these sensations are simply part of our world. In Eurhythmics class all students, even the very young, are trained to listen carefully. "Listen to the sound of the triangle. Hear it getting softer and softer. Put your hands up when the sound starts and keep them up until the sound is gone." Children and adults find this experience fascinating and they listen intently. "Feel how light your legs are when you skip. Feel how heavy your legs are when you push them into the floor of mud." Such imagery arouses strong sensations by stimulating not only visual impressions but also a recollection of physical sensations. These sensations can be evoked by music. We listen to a concert and find dramatic images coming back from memory. They may have no direct connection with the current music but arise from old and distant associations between music and movement.

We have been fortunate to work with two talented teachers of body movement who use imagery to help people move more freely. Theater instructor Sally Sykes gave us an evocative picture of a cloak falling behind us as we walked—a cape made of heavy velvet brocade, trailing on the ground. We responded to the image with a walk that was slow, proud, and erect. The immense weight of the cape pulling at the shoulders that demanded a certain forward force necessary to maintain balance. A moment later she changed the picture to a scarf of chiffon, floating in the breeze as we walked along the edge of a grassy cliff. A noticeable difference came over our whole musculature—a feeling of ease and flexibility with a light step. Our walking speed increased and we felt an immense pleasure in simply moving. When we experience such vivid imagery with our bodies we feel a strong sensory arousal. The ability to invoke the sensation through our own movement, feeling the difference in the quick change from heavy to light, is a far more intense experience than merely visualizing the image in our minds.

The most memorable imagery from George Lewis's body movement classes involved a big, fat crayon. Imagine the crayon tied to the end of a stick strapped to your head. Using this crayon, write your full name on the ceiling. The stick suddenly moves from your head to your elbow, and you draw circles on one wall, then another. This peripatetic stick may appear on your knee, your hip, or your shoulder—always with a job to perform. The physical flexibility this moving image demands is astonishing. Muscles you were unaware of are brought into play. Self-consciousness goes out the window, while everyone in the class concentrates and laughs.

Multimodal Memory

Dalcroze work aims to make us more aware of all the senses operating and cooperating at any given moment. Adding new activities makes us increasingly cognizant of each new task. For instance, we begin with listening, add walking, and then singing. We watch the movements of our classmates and cooperate with their changing positions. Storing episodes in each mode gives us more sensations for recall. The retrieval process is like that of an assembly room, where plans for what will take place, in what order, and with what energy level are determined and reviewed "just prior to shipment."

Drawing on various memories, the mind evaluates options and predicts outcomes the instant before commands are sent to the sensory system and executed by the muscles. The value of several modes functioning at once was apparent in an experiment I conducted with advanced piano students. When asked to play a Bach fugue (even more complex than a canon) from memory, they could easily accomplish this on the computer-based keyboard used for the experiment. Even when the computer scrambled the pitches so that the keys no longer corresponded to the expected notes, the students could still play their fugue! How could they do this? They reported that the moment they realized what was happening, they turned off the sound coming into their ears and listened to the sound in their memory. The internal sound came moments before the external sound traveling along their aural system; the internal sound guided their fingers to play the correct key patterns. Their kinesthetic memory carried a portion of responsibility for this accomplishment—the fingers moved almost on automatic pilot.

When the same students tried to play *America* on the electronically altered keyboard, they had much more difficulty. Under ordinary circumstances, they played this song by ear. They were accustomed to improvising the accompaniments, and consequently did not have a set series of fixed finger and arm positions. The kinesthetic sequences were not well established in their memories. Without these kinesthetic sequences, the string of sounds of *America* in their aural memory was not strong enough to assure a reliable performance.

Multimodal learning in Dalcroze classes employs more than proprioceptive and aural stimulation. Bright scarves used in movement activities engage students' visual sense. Music notation is also visual. Teachers often use—and encourage students to use—graphic notation. These simple line drawings express the flow, energy, and direction of music. Various techniques of touching and rubbing hand drums involve the tactile sense, thereby providing students with still another type of memory to intensify a specific experience.

Students may store impressions of short and long in numerous ways: they tap a rhythmic pattern including a long note on a drum, using a rubbing glide for the long note; they step the pattern and make a stretch for the long note; they swish a scarf for quick notes and make an arc across the ceiling for the long note; or they draw a series of strokes followed by an extended line for the long note. Their recall of this concept of short and long will be very dependable because of their proprioceptive experience. It will be an internal representation—a prototype—that they can apply to music, athletics, speech, and design.

Muscle Memory

Habituation and automatisms (automatic actions) are devices Dalcroze teachers utilize to expand the complexity of students' activities. Repetition, with variations that keep attention high, quickly develops a stable and reliable memory of a certain movement pattern. Successive repetitions follow the cycle of stimulus, perception, storage, and retrieval, thereby creating a nearly automatic path of recall that is successful even in times of stress. When movements are added, students continue to perform the automatism along with the new movements.

This muscle memory is an indispensable tool for everyday living. After we take our second step walking up a stairway, our muscle memory will have established a standard measurement that our body expects to repeat until it arrives at the top. Our skill at calculating this distance is so refined that even the slightest difference in riser-height can result in a fall. If the step is higher than we expect, we catch a toe and lose our balance; if it is lower, our foot slips and shakes our composure. This is why we can effortlessly carry on a conversation while we walk up the steps of public buildings. Construction law requires that the steps be exactly the same height. On the other hand, when we descend along a pathway of stepping stones, our attention is so occupied with judging space and conscious movement that our conversational brilliance may fade a bit.

Without the phenomenon of muscle memory we could not develop complex skills. Any typist or musician can provide testimony. In the early learning stage of a new craft, muscle memory is virtually non-existent because there are few memory connections to make appropriate links. With every repetition, more connections are made until the pattern of movement is easy to retrieve. One movement memory pulls along the next one, and then the next. This muscle memory can continue with little attention. I remember once falling asleep at the piano, only to pop back to consciousness a moment or two later. I realized my hands had continued moving and were several lines farther along in the music! There was no attention from my conscious mind—motor memory alone accomplished this.

Internalized Sensations

> Music training should develop inner hearing—that is, the capacity for distinctly hearing music mentally as well as physically.[7]

Sometimes internal images appear in our minds by what seems to be an involuntary stimulation. We can be startled by sudden flashes of personal history that appear "on their own" without a conscious trigger. Errant electrical impulses in our brain can stir up long dormant memories and dump them, in vivid color, onto the floor of our consciousness. More useful is the ability to search consciously in our memory for images and sensations. Those images with strong internal representations can easily be recalled in moments of quiet reflection, without overt movement or stimulation. Once recalled, they can be considered, connected to other thoughts, or used to guide future action.

As a composer, Dalcroze knew that the internal sense of sound was the spawning ground of musical invention. As a teacher he endeavored to strengthen his students' internal music images so that they could create in their imagination fresh combinations of sounds, rhythms, melodies, textures, timbres, patterns, and forms.

Performing musicians listen internally to the sound of a learned composition so they can experiment in their mind with various phrasings, intensities, and tempi. Without the distraction of technique, musicians have the freedom to concentrate on musical flow. With ample practice in listening internally they are ready at performance time to evoke a strong internal sense of the beginning tempo, the dynamic quality of the entrance, and the length of breath needed for the first phrase. Likewise, dancers and actors prepare themselves just before their entrance by imagining a sense of the opening activity "in full color"—the color of all the senses.

Dalcroze games develop their participants' internal sense of sound. Using a Quick Reaction approach, Dalcroze would instruct students to stop singing a known melody aloud and continue singing the melody internally until the next command. At the next command, all would sing aloud again. If the students' internal images of the melody were reliable and their concentration was high, they would succeed in returning on the correct tone, at the correct place in the melody, in unison!

A frequent activity in Dalcroze classes is to begin with large movements expressing some basic aspect of music, perhaps a sway from side to side with matching arm swings. Gradually the size of the movements becomes smaller along with the amount of energy used and the parts of the body involved. The torso becomes quiet, then the shoulders, arms, wrists, and hands—until the entire body is absolutely still. At this point the inner spirit is aware of the rhythmic sensation, throbbing internally and making its lasting imprint in memory.

By swaying at varying degrees of energy and with different parts of the body (arms, wrists, fingers), we experience subtle differentiations of the sensations of weight, energy, time, and space. When we recall "sway," all the experiences stored in our memories are stimulated creating a powerful revival of the sway sensation. Dalcroze's ultimate goal in movement work was to develop this capacity to recall vividly any musical sensation from within oneself.

We can apply this augmented capacity for sensation to all incoming information and impressions. Within ourselves we have the potential to see worlds in our imaginations and to hear whole symphonies in our heads. Without the fibers pressing against our skin, we can perceive the touch of silk—our memories let us feel it. Our limbs remember how the material slipped through our finger joints. We recall the gentle motions of our elbows as we swished the fabric back and forth. We can "touch" the coldness of steel through the proprioceptive memory of the degree of tension in a shoulder, ready to lift a hand away if the steel is too cold to tolerate. We can "smell" the scent of rose water or chicken on the grill without the odors actually being in the air aound us. Part of these sensory memories come from the proprioceptive sensations of body posture as we lean over a bottle to sniff the rose water or lift the chicken onto a plate. By focusing on these internal body sensations, we can greatly enrich our sensory consciousness.

When we can arouse sensations by an internal command, we are no longer dependent upon external stimulation. We are ready to play with images in our head, forming new associations with other memories, enlarging some aspects and diminishing others. This is the creative process underlying the imagination.

Action

The learning and memory systems just discussed are what we draw upon to take effective action. Eurhythmics enriches our powers of imagination, which in turn, give us the tools to express ourselves through improvisation—the ultimate aim of an accomplished Eurhythmician. The nature of this training in improvisation extends far beyond the musical realm and greatly enriches our daily lives.

Imagination

Imagination is composed of the sensations the mind has had the privilege, opportunity, or misfortune to collect. A flexible mind combines and re-combines sensations in various ways and creates imagined scenarios. We need not travel to the tropics to imagine lying on a beach beside a blue ocean. While a photograph may present some visual clues, this is a superficial level of experience. Adding the sensation of the sun's warmth, the graininess of the sand, the enfolding quality of the water, and the relaxation of muscles and joints when lying down, we can arouse a richer experience. Multiple body sensations must be aroused to gain—or regain—the full effect of the memory. Only with active sensation can we guide the developing image into an organic whole. If we create images based on cognition alone—named objects and their relationships—our creations will be half-alive, missing subtleties that our senses add.

Dalcroze tapped the power of imagination with every method he could devise. He deplored the practice of asking students for only mimicking response. He preferred to challenge students with situations where they must invent their response.

> We are too apt to appeal to the child's instinct for imitation to the detriment of his sense of analysis and his inventive faculties ... The child loves nothing so much as to construct and embellish according to his fancy things that appeal to him. Similarly, he wants lessons that give scope for his individuality.[8]

When the simple activity of tapping knees in time with the music changes to the teacher's challenge to, "Find another place to tap," the students become the initiators. They are in control of the moment and they are responsible for the successful continuation of class activities. Students search their internal image of "body" to find places on their body that they can reach and tap. They must remember what places have already been tapped—the instruction is to find a different place—and they must move quickly to stay in rhythm with the music.

Activities like these involve imagination, initiative, and rapid decision-making. Every change of movement revitalizes the physical sensation of rhythm. Students might show the increasing energy of a crescendo (music gradually becoming louder) by raising their arms, spreading their arms wide, rising on their toes, or assuming a drooping posture that unfolds as the energy of the music pushes them upwards. With these abundant sensations successfully stored in memory, they develop a large vocabulary to use creatively.

Dalcroze used exercises to broaden students' capacity for seeing and employing alternatives. The value of generating choices was tested in an experiment with school children:

> The children were asked to list all the uses they could think of for a piece of paper, a car, etc. After the program these children produced more original responses to new problems and made larger gains in reading comprehension and solving word problems in mathematics than similar control students. It was also noted that children who were identified as behavior problems were more attentive to their teachers and their studies and with better results than similar control students. The extensive response suggests that gain may have resulted from motivational as well as, or in addition to, specific training in generating responses. The experiment students were also found to be showing marked degrees of improvement ten months after the experiment had ended.[9]

Improvisation

Dalcroze believed improvisation to be the pinnacle of musician-ship. He saw Eurhythmics and Solfege as tools in the creative process of musical improvisation. Expressing oneself in music is a form of communication that is individual, intimate, and when done well, capable of touching the emotions of others.

Improvising requires initiating action rather than responding to someone else's command; it is an activity that affirms our individuality. The impulse and the realization come from inside the improviser with "impulse" as the critical element. Improvising flows from moment to moment, each moment growing out of the previous activity. We find the next step although we are not sure what the next step should be. It requires sizing up the situation, trusting our judgments, and acting upon our assessments.

Improvisation occurs daily in many ways. A conversation is an improvisation, unless we have prepared a speech. As we speak, we pull together the words that express the images, emotions, and thoughts in our mind. There is probably no field of activity where improvisation does not occur. Ingenious, impromptu bits of activity often times divert disaster. We freely improvise in the kitchen. Not enough lettuce? Make a relish dish of crisp veggies. No sour cream, but—aha!—yogurt with a dash of curry powder, soy sauce, and mustard! Skilled improvisation requires a vision of what needs to happen and the ability to assemble the needed resources.

The resources for improvisation are stored as the sensations, the connections, and the constructs in our memories. Improvisation excites the memory traces in a most lively way, alerting everything available. It is as if confetti has just been wafted into the air and we are catching pieces that seem to fit together as they drift downward.

Time is an essential element in musical improvisation. When we open to the whole world of knowledge (and we need to do this to explore the maximum number of choices) we cannot review every item with equal consideration. The rational planning part of our mind must back off and give control to the music impulse. Because the outcome is unplanned, there is always risk involved. As Herb Henke said:

> At first I was terribly worried about how it would come out. Now I can just go to the piano, sit down, and not think ahead of time. I put my hands down and begin to come up with what I want to do. If I'm going into a class in which I must improvise a great deal and I haven't been at the keyboard at all, well, it may work out, it may not. If I'm in my studio and I practice a great deal, it's usually not so good. If you try to re-create what you've done in class—then you can't succeed. But if you just open the door and say 'Yes I'm in a milieu,' or 'This is a comfortable key today,' you find yourself open and ready to go.

Marjalena Juntenan, of Finland, noticed the effects of learning improvisation in Dalcroze classes:

> What was revolutionary for me was the improvising. I was very shy in improvising, but beginning with the movement improvisation, I opened up a lot. After a year or so I really learned to enjoy it. I had the feeling that I can do it, and I can be good at it. Even though what everyone did was different, whatever I did was also good.

The success of improvisation depends on the strength and flexibility of the imagination—its capacity to hold and rearrange impressions from memory. If the memories can be recalled with considerable detail, the improviser can make choices and shape the results with continuity and skill.

Most improvisation operates within some external design. Jazz relies mainly on the harmonies of popular songs. A Dalcroze teacher's improvisations are shaped by the musical task at hand. Church organists' interludes are bound by the key and character of the service. Musicians playing for fashion shows and wedding receptions may have restrictions in the mood of the music, although they may be totally free in all other choices.

Because there is no prescribed choreography in Eurhythmics classes, the students must improvise their own movements to represent how the music "looks." Of course, some of the decisions are guided by the music, but others arise from within the individual.

A good teacher in any classroom must develop the ability to improvise, no matter what the subject. A teacher who takes cues from student responses can make on-the-spot revisions that catch what the students have expressed and guide it through an improvised route to the target of the lesson.

Dalcroze emphasized improvisation as the essential skill for those training to be teachers of his method. He stressed the necessity to improvise music that expressed the desired sensation so unmistakably that an attentive student could not miss it. Above all, he insisted that the improvising be musical: that it be rhythmically performed, with gradations of tone, variations in energy, and good phrasing. Marie-Laure Bachmann, Director the Jaques-Dalcroze Institute in Geneva, shows how much the expressiveness of the improvisation matters. When she was working as a music therapist, she arrived late one evening worn out from the day's activities to work with Gabriel (one of her patients). Gabriel was not responding well and the lesson was not productive. Finally Gabriel said, "Well, how can I do my exercises well when you play so badly?" Marie-Laure took that outspoken remark as a justified observation. She had let her fatigue overcome her sensitivity and the patient responded accordingly. She said, "A teacher's music must arouse and fit the feeling. One must always give the children a musical atmosphere."

As Dalcroze stressed, the essence of improvisation is the intimate two-way connection between imagination and execution:

Rhythmic gymnastics accomplishes both...intellectual and physical development. How? By constantly demanding conscious implementation of thought. Hear a musical thought? Express it in movement. Make a series of movements, express it in music.[10]

While there are many reliable paths for emotional, physical, mental, and spiritual areas of growth, Eurhythmics is a most exhilarating way to experience such expansion. Feeling yourself wholly involved—mind concentrating, body demonstrating, heart full of sensitivity, in synchronization with beautiful music—sets a condition of *being* that is accessible to all, transferable to other endeavors, and renewable throughout one's life.

CHAPTER SIX

PERSONAL TESTIMONIES

"[Eurhythmics creates] a sense of being part of something wonderful, a great world all working together harmoniously."AM*

In the last fifty years, our knowledge about how we operate—what makes us go—has rapidly accumulated. Amazing devices allow us to watch the brain functioning while we read a book, recite poetry, or listen to music. We are becoming ever more certain about where the brain processes various stimuli, how long it takes sensory responses to reach various locations in the brain, and how long it takes to react under diverse conditions. Modern research confirms what Dalcroze suspected: movement stimulates the mind and emotions, affecting subsequent thoughts and judgments. Similarly, posture, movements, and mental imaging influence emotional states.

A focal point of the interviews for this book is how Eurhythmics changes the way we feel about ourselves. The three aspects of body, mind, and spirit often come together as participants report how changes in one area relate to changes in another. Students who make physical improvements say they feel less shy and mentally more confident. Some respondents participated in

*See Appendix A for the names of respondents identified in this chapter by their initials.

Eurhythmics for years with little sense of positive mental growth until they experienced a spiritual awakening, an epiphany, or a reason to live, provoking changes in their thoughts and actions.

One respondent, talking about the effect of Eurhythmics, declared it was, "Losing inhibitions. Not worrying that somebody is watching. I realized that nobody is looking—it's all me, within myself, and I can just do what I can do, and nobody is going to correct me." Each student strives to listen and sense, intent upon expressing the flow of music as sensitively as possible. Of course, teachers are looking—that is essential to the development of the class—but there is no "social" looking. Students move according to their personal relationship to the music, giving and receiving within the freedom of individual movement. There are right and wrong activities such as conducting in 2-meter when the music is in 3-meter but these parts of the experience are side issues to the central understanding that we are free to let our bodies respond to the music as we feel it.

Throughout the interviews, such words as "joy," "concentration," "awareness," "feeling," "flow," "open," "happiness," and "energy," recur. They adorn the descriptions of personal growth. While personal progression need not be linear, Eurhythmics classes progress from physical to mental to spiritual. Classes begin with students moving to music, then gradually involve the mind through responding to verbal and musical commands, and after repeated exercises and musical challenges, stimulate a growth many express as spiritual. Eurhythmics provides a fresh way to see the world, a feeling of deeper respect for others, and a desire to be more open and giving.

PHYSICAL

Three main themes emerge in this physical area: becoming aware of one's body, becoming aware of the space in which the body moves, and becoming aware of the quality of movement. Most respondents speak of becoming aware of their bodies for the first time in their lives. One person stated that, finally, after persistent work, "My body is part of me and my experience."[AD] While this remark may seem trivial, the harmonious experience of a united body and mind evades many people.

Many practitioners express prior embarrassment with their bodies, perhaps due to spiritual beliefs that the body is unclean or due to cultural stereotypes that their particular body size and shape is imperfect. One participant rediscovered the "joy of moving. I did not remember what it was like."[AS] While these same feelings might be realized through structured dance classes, some dancers believe that Dalcroze methods finally helped them accept their bodies. One woman who trained early in her life as a dancer still felt uneasy about her body despite the fact that she learned to dance to music. She had merely learned the steps as technique, following the technical dictates without inner feeling or personal involvement. She describes her experience of Eurhythmics as a "move to light."[HvM] Eurhythmics offered her the chance to move with an inner conviction—she physically and emotionally connected to the experience of moving with music, expressing her own inner state.

One college student recalls that she was so shy about her body she was afraid to be seen by the teacher. She said, "I hoped all those moving bodies between me and the instructor would protect me from scrutiny and criticism."[KW] Through Eurhythmics, she gradually gained confidence in her body and soon felt free to move about the room with ease.

> I remember discovering the joy of movement through Eurhythmics. [The instructor] played for us to move, turned us loose to run, run, leap about in the room. It was fun! We began to smile and laugh with each other like children too long made to sit still and be quiet. It evoked the feeling of

freedom I had as a small child leaping and running in the grass, lost in the joy of movement. This feeling stayed with me very strongly. Later in my life, I would run, run, leap up and down the deserted sidewalk, trying to recapture the joy of that afternoon.[KW]

Along with a newfound body awareness, many express a deepening appreciation of the surrounding physical space. Once participants become cognizant of their personal space, the possibilities of extending their bodies into the environment are exhilarating and exciting. Repeatedly they describe their personal growth in terms of becoming "open." An older participant said that over the years she had experienced a continual opening of her body which had previously felt "closed."[HvM] For others the sense of openness translated into a mental feeling of ease, "I feel more comfortable to sing, move, and improvise."[CM] Another said, "You feel more like you want to be. I feel more open to different types of people and subjects."

The combination of bodily and spatial awareness allow students to focus on improving the quality of their movement. Prior to their Dalcroze experience, negative self images drove many to seek improvement in their external physical appearance. After Eurhythmics, they shifted their focus to improve themselves at a deeper level, "When you feel your whole body you can get into your inner feeling without embarrassment."[JLAP]

For some, Eurhythmics helps overcome physical ailments caused by congenital problems, accidents, or, in the case of musicians, detrimental techniques on the instrument. The following testimony is from a person who had undergone back surgery:

I had worried and even been warned that I would have to give up my former athletic life, my love of modern and folk dance, and my attachment to all things physical. The concentration necessary for a Eurhythmics class helped me focus on the task at hand. I learned to move with less fear, therefore less pain.

The necessity to use mind, body, and emotion together increased my interest in integrated body.[TeB]

In a most remarkable story, a student who survived a life threatening car accident credits her recovery to work done in Eurhythmics. When she awoke from unconsciousness after the accident, she could breathe only with great difficulty, she could not concentrate, she had lost a keen sense of balance, and she had poor memory skills. Her doctor advised her to study Eurhythmics. Within one year she claimed that she was ninety percent recovered. In the New York Dalcroze School under Hilda Schuster, she practiced stepping to the beat while using arm beats to show the musical measure. After she mastered this task, she learned to perform the arm beats in canon, where the teacher plays a pattern and the students must then demonstrate the same pattern a number of beats later: "Without doing the arm beats in canon, I could not do what I can do now. It helped in my sense of balance very much. Being in balance is like a canon; your body is doing several things at once to adjust."[MSh]

Another student suffered for years with various physical injuries that prevented her from playing the violin. After two years of Dalcroze instruction she was able to master her injuries. She credits Eurhythmics with making her mindful that she must play the violin with the whole body—not just the smaller muscles that she overworked to the point of fatigue. Additionally, the Dalcroze work gave her the confidence to perform again with the belief that, "I have a right to be here. My body is as good as anyone else's."[AD]

More and more, Dalcroze grasped that the conditioning of the human body, its health and care, is vitally important for any kind of performance. He urged educators and parents alike to become concerned with the development of their children, including developing physical skills. To Dalcroze, healthy development included music, attention to breath control, and coordination of various muscle groups to refine control while still retaining elegance, all with no wasted energy. Music ensured the proper growth in a well-ordered atmosphere. There were patterns for the mind to appreciate, varying spaces and energies for the body to express, and fluctuations of spirit for emotional stimulation and regulation.

LETTING GO MENTALLY

Overwhelmingly, respondents state that the Eurhythmics experience helps them feel more whole. They talk about the sense of connecting their left to their right brain and feeling more balanced and centered. One person describes this sense of entirety as "pleasuring the accountant." This description captures the dualistic nature of the calculating rational side of our brain and the free uninhibited side. Some interviewees overcame debilitating weaknesses in their concentration, their memory, and their interpersonal skills. The following response illustrates how letting go mentally results in a feeling of deep satisfaction:

> How well I remember the first time I was doing something very rhythmically complex between hands and feet in an advanced class improvisation. I realized that the cognitive (left) brain had no idea what I was doing—could not visualize it in notation. This was a wholly right brain experience and very exhilarating![CA]

When someone says, "You are thinking too much—learn to live day to day," or "Concentrate on the present," they are referring to our tendency to emphasize the rational mind over the intuitive mind. Many of our respondents became aware of such an imbalance during Eurhythmics exercises. While stepping to the beat of the music, a verbal or musical cue might tell us to change direction. Our mind says, "Which way do I go?" but the beat of the music does not give us time to think. In an instant we are off on a new path, carried along by the enjoyable sounds. Yes, we have engaged both mind and body, and the two have acted as one. We have struck a beautiful balance.

In a recent Eurhythmics session, I experienced a similar breakthrough. The teacher performed pairs of music intervals—perfect fifths and major seconds. The students were grouped in pairs and each member of the pair was assigned one of the two intervals. When an interval was sounded the designated person made a gesture for that interval. At first the tempo was slow and each participant had time to listen carefully to each sound before reacting. However, as the speed increased each person had to react so quickly that the time to think was curtailed. Soon the couples were moving less stiffly and were creating a flow between one another. The thinking brain was no longer leading; the mind and body were moving as one. There was a sense of smoothness and clarity. All nervous energy was lost in the flow of the dance.

INTEGRATION OF MIND AND BODY

One young woman describes her awareness of body and mind successfully working together. "I feel the integration of all parts moving together, and flexibility in making choices. When working in music I have a feeling of being 'in' the music."[UH] Another student credits Dalcroze work leading to a deeper appreciation of music: "I gained an understanding of music that music theory classes hadn't given me. It was on a more intuitive and feeling level combined with the intellectual."[MSz]

After much work in Eurhythmics, many find a sense of wholeness, along with a renewed vigor in their art. They are able to use this energy to find more pleasure in music and they can transfer this enthusiasm to their students and others. Dominique Porte, retired head of the Jaques Dalcroze Institute in Geneva, describes how the improvement in his piano playing continued throughout his life because of "better listening, economy of forces, phrasing, and emotionality." These internal characteristics are the heart of musical expression—aided by technique but not generated by technique. Dalcroze searched for this same musical flow in his students a hundred years ago.

CONCENTRATION

Musicians perform several tasks at the same time. An organist plays with both hands and feet; a conductor aurally differentiates the French horns from the first violins. These skills are vital in everyday life as well—the ability to catch ourselves from slipping on the ice as we balance the shovel, or the capacity to carry on a conversation while driving on a busy street. These aptitudes can be developed with practice. Rather than expressing frustration at such challenges, Eurhythmicians experience the thrill of trying to accomplish them.

> "The Dalcroze work is so intense. There are so many things you have to do at one time that you can't let your mind go on anything else—anything at all. You have to concentrate. You can't daydream. You must be ready to respond." [BPH]

> "What I really learned that you have to do in Eurhythmics is concentrate on what's coming and then move your body— being able to concentrate on change and not have the body involved in the concentration." [MJ]

SOCIAL INTEGRATION

Dalcroze believed in the power of Eurhythmics to direct us toward social integration. He designed games so that his students would develop a sense of mutual support. Students work to share both the responsibilities and the delights.

The first thought I have is to be open to other people. The music is the main element, but there is also socialization that for me is the way to become open. Eurhythmics opened me to other people's energy. I can cooperate with people who are different from me because Eurhythmics brings so many different things into balance. Maybe we don't choose to do work with these people in our lives, but when we are in the same room with the music we can do things together.[SM]

Another interviewee spoke of personal growth from sharing the process of creation:

It has everything to do with internal awareness. Yesterday I was doing improvisation with someone, hands together, sensitive to who would move first. I did similar exercises years ago, wanting everything to turn out "right," wanting people to notice that it was right, and therefore taking over and controlling the exercise. Yesterday I just did the exercise, letting the other person know it was okay to wait, to go, and so on, without losing it ... Since you're doing these exercises in a group and other people are doing them as well, earlier I would have fallen into thinking, "I'm good, I'm better than the others." In Eurhythmics I get this immediate physical good feeling, without feeling better than other people. You're not the star of the show.[AC]

A key to personal growth in Eurhythmics centers around limiting the negative power of the ego. Through the games and activities, we lose some of that competitive sense of "beating out" others for our own gain. In the process, we find ourselves anew with greater confidence and resolve. Expressing his search for honesty in redefining himself, Abbott Chrisman remarks on the value of positive feedback on personal growth:

There is the issue of giving up control—giving up the intellectual notion of what is good (acceptance and humility). A really interesting element of the internal self-consciousness is that, generally speaking, only positive reinforcement is used.

It starts with the earliest good feeling that you get from managing to pass the ball in fours while you're stepping twos. We leave negative events alone because they simply do not provide a good feeling. The system operates by continuously reinforcing the positive. As Aristotle says, learning feels good.

Another student tells of the importance of maintaining a positive attitude towards other class members: "An individual's attitude toward the others in the class is important," observed Sylvie Morgenegg. "We learn to regulate our energy; it is a way to natural self-control. It would be misplaced if you left the classroom thinking, 'I was right, I did the right thing.'" For Eurhythmicians, being "correct" is unimportant; being "present" is the valuable gain. In the same vein, Abbott felt that "getting something that is basic right gives a feeling of being good without feeling better than other people." He added that he progressed beyond a physical level of right and wrong to a spiritual understanding: "I used to do it all intellectually. Slowly, step by step it has been possible (not only on a physical level of text but on a practical and a spiritual level of right and wrong) to trust and to be open to sensation."

Today in elementary schools educators are increasingly considering the importance of what Daniel Goldman calls "emotional intelligence." Social integration develops from non-verbal communication (in the form of movement) rather than from spoken communication. For example, at the Nueva Learning Center, an innovative school in San Francisco, students in the fifth grade take a course called Self Science. In one particular exercise, students form teams and put together a jigsaw puzzle where each must communicate in order to fit certain given pieces together. However, the rules of the game are that there can be no talking or gesturing. While this type of cooperation has always taken place in team sports it is interesting that this idea is now being valued in the academic setting.[1]

INTERACTION

Dalcroze classes use games to encourage social interaction. Two students share a drum and tap out patterns to each other—changing tempo, dynamics and articulation in a conversational way. Students form groups and are assigned specific phrases from a composition to perform in sequence. Each group moves in a pattern and manner to carry the sense of the music to the next group. The social effort of harmonizing into a single expression brings people out of themselves into a dynamic relationship with the others in the class and with the music.

While teaching accompaniment at the Geneva Conservatory, Sylvie Morgenegg and her students attended classes in movement at the Dalcroze Institute. Many of them felt insecure when playing accompaniment for dancers. Watching Dalcroze students move in their naturally rhythmic way, the music students gradually gained confidence as performers. "They picked up the energy from the dancers, and realized they played much better when looking at the dancers. They felt energy and they gave energy back."

Dominique Porte noted that one of the delights of teaching Eurhythmics was the joy of playing for others. The "lonesome vice" of piano playing became a means of working with people and sharing the joy of music. He also expressed his conviction that music has the power to better human life. Its purpose is "to move us" and that purpose alone makes it worth doing.

CHAMBER MUSIC

For musicians, playing chamber music is one of the most thrilling forms of musical communication, with all players listening intently to each other. Each player is keenly aware of the others' entrances and phrases, noting the tempo, stresses, nuances, colorings, and breath. An essential ingredient for success is the group's ability to accept and encourage another's musical ideas. Dalcroze trained his students for this kind of interaction by focusing on one another's movements; then modeling, copying, and communicating at a profound level that transcends personality clashes.

Playing chamber music requires particularly sensitive listening. Eurhythmics heightened the inner power of my musical movement and led me to a greater sympathy for the movements of others. I started to sense other's movements as my own. Indeed, I learned that as a musician I needed this skill to properly converse with people through music.

SENSITIVE PHRASING

Good communication of any kind can benefit by sensitive phrasing. The psychologist Frank Restle, who often drew upon his understanding of music and music performance in his writings, wrote:

> Phrasing is effective in making the structure of a pattern easier to comprehend. This suggests that phrasing and rhythm in speech and music are not only a matter of personal style but also may have an important bearing on the intelligibility not in the mere sense of word recognition but in the larger sense of communication of ideas...[Experiments show] that putting relatively long pauses between major divisions and shorter pauses between minor parts of a pattern can enhance the observer's ability to perceive and anticipate the sequence, and pauses placed in conflict with the natural structure of the pattern may be quite harmful.[2]

Restle hit upon a vital characteristic of good chamber music—the musical thoughts must be phrased so expressively that the other players can understand and carry on the conversation. Any performance between several people excels when each player finishes a phrase with the impression of having expressed a statement, remains quietly alert while others play and re-enters at exactly the right moment with a new breath. The split second accuracy of a quartet may not be necessary for all our communications. But clear statements, attentive silence while others speak, and striving for mutually satisfying conclusions can occur in nonmusical interactions when we cooperate like a musical quartet.

COOPERATION AND CONFIDENCE

Dalcroze, as a composer and performing musician, understood well the special character of communication through music. He saw this as an essential skill to be developed during a child's upbringing:

> As the child feels himself delivered from all physical embarrassment and mental obsession of a lower order, added to the sense—acquired by the practice of combining his individual efforts with those of the rest of the class—of participation in a collective movement, he will conceive a profound joy of an elevated character, a new factor in ethical progress, a new stimulus to will power.[3] . . . I call the joy "elevated" because it will not be based on external circumstances. It will be distinct from pleasure in that it becomes a permanent condition of the being, independent alike of time and of the events that have given rise to it, an integral element of our organism. It will flower in the hidden recesses of the soul, where the vigor [energy] of our individuality is [formed and released] secreted, a vigor . . . which may be applied in every direction and never be depleted.[4]

One respondent (MHA) noted a strong connection between Eurhythmics and the principles later developed by Piaget, especially the thesis that areas in the brain are not awake until they are stimulated by movement. Movement is essential to the development of imagination. During their first year of class children have strongly varying temperaments; by their second year they are learning to give and take in their groups. This social aspect is very important, she says, and especially clear to see in children.

SPIRITUAL GROWTH

Eurhythmicians gain confidence as they become aware of their body and its connection to their mind. Many also find that their behavior toward others is enriched. Some describe these changes in ways we reserve for discussing the spiritual parts of our lives. One person described her revelations in Eurhythmics by saying, "I experienced a move toward light."[HvM]

In tandem with physical and mental growth, many experience a spiritual awakening within themselves. This often involves conquering fears about their own worth as human beings and their life purpose. In addition, respondents speak about their desire to integrate themselves into society in a positive way. Others speak of a zeal to share the benefits of Eurhythmics by teaching and speaking about the Dalcroze method.

The experience I related earlier about observing children on a playground and then improvising music from their movements deeply moved me. After this particular assignment, I became aware of the spiritual side to this study. This understanding developed slowly over the years. At the time of this experience—feeling those basic movements of swinging on a swing, lifting a toy shovel, and bouncing a ball—the world was teaming with meaning. I moved with an enhanced perception; the various angles and straight lines in the still life meant more. Buildings and man-made objects transmitted emotions and ideas; I realized that the buildings were the "frozen" forms of human feelings.

A DIRECTION FOR LIFE

The following quotations from several outstanding Dalcroze teachers express a belief in the power of Eurhythmics so strong that it caused a reorientation of their life's course in order to spread the benefits of the method to others.

I felt the importance of this training so intensely that, in fact, I married it! I was engaged to marry but my fiancé expected me to stay home and give up my teaching. I said, "No, I've got to justify what I vowed to my mother; I've got to justify that I can give something."[PH]

Dalcroze Eurhythmics, in short, unleashed my enthusiasm. I was a believer. I never lost an opportunity to explain to a mother or father what their child was learning, what the benefits of the class were, and to encourage people to continue. I was an advertising agency, not for myself, but for something I believed in. It was something that had really helped me and changed the children I taught.[TeB]

We seek the harmonization of the human being. And ten years ago I was embarrassed to talk about this because I thought it was too holy, holy. But not any more. I don't feel any awkwardness. Now I can say that to you, and I can see the effect in my life too. I seem to have learned a technique in my life with which I can reach some people's hearts and souls and give them harmony.[GC]

For some practitioners, Eurhythmics becomes the foundation for the guiding principles in their lives.

I find in the exercises sensitivity toward the presence of others. They facilitate us in real life to be with others. There is a power in music to unify different elements in a pleasant and creative manner. Since I started the research on Dalcroze, professional success in a social sense does not interest me anymore. My concern now is how far I can succeed in exploiting my personal faculties (myself as one human being in a group of people). In a sense, I learned to be free from any personal attachment in respecting myself as well as others. To search for liberty all one's life is the most essential. Dalcroze's philosophy is based on this notion, I believe.[ToB]

STRENGTH AND FLEXIBILITY IN TIMES OF CRISIS

Perhaps the most dramatic story of the spiritual benefits of Eurhythmics is from a woman (JEK) who had recently divorced and lost all of her monetary resources. Eurhythmics, she says, helped her find a way to put order into her carefree existence, where she paid little attention to the ramifications of her actions. She described her realizations as an epiphany. From this centered, structured place, she was able to write five books. Once she developed the skills to manage her own affairs, she was able to teach more effectively. She has also been able to bring these skills to her interpersonal relations and is now leading a confident and more productive life.

The move outward from this inner confidence leads many to develop a deeper sense of empathy toward others. It is impossible to authentically extend ourselves to others until we have discovered our own personal center and balance. "For one partner in a couple to truly empathize with the other demands that his own emotional reactions calm down to the point where he is able to mirror the feelings of his partner. Without this physiological attunement, a partner's sense of what the other is feeling is likely to be entirely off base."[5]

A mother found that Eurhythmics helped her handle family relationships more effectively. Having been very shy, she credits Eurhythmics with forcing her to become less inhibited; she talks about becoming much more confident and assertive. Yet she balances these feelings with the realization that, "You are rather small in terms of everything else." Referring to her musical development, she states, "I learned so much about feeling the phrasing and nuance, and the feeling of line. It was a very enriching experience as a student." Then came the application to other facets of her life. "You grow tremendously. I began to see what was happening with myself and the children. I was able to stand back more and I became less selfish. I was able to handle confrontations effectively."[AS]

As different parts of the brain are stimulated by Dalcroze activities, many people also discover they are able to find more options in solving problems. They can access their imaginative powers and see solutions that otherwise might be missed.

OPENING TO THE WORLD

Two more responses show how Dalcroze teaching leads people to develop very strong beliefs in the power of music. Both are a testament to the depth of awareness that occurs with musicians who have been practicing their art for years.

> The Dalcroze teaching goes beyond the Eurhythmics class into transcending what could be an otherwise boring life. The "gifts" around us at some point originate from movement, the essence of life itself. I have never been led to this awareness by any other medium. Because the Dalcroze work deals with the complete human body as an instrument, it is almost as if the human body itself becomes a "university," a medium or gift for discovering the natural world around us in order to create our own music.[MB]

> The main discovery for me, in this new life I started with learning and teaching Eurhythmics, is the discovery of music as a language, a life, individual and social. Music is, to me, the inner perception, the inner movement I can share with others, leading us toward the true feeling and knowledge of what we are, and of what we should be.[DP]

HAPPINESS AND JOY

Dalcroze was a great educator who knew that if the exercises were enjoyable, students would more easily remember the concepts. Although his exercises could be very challenging, they were also fun. The mind stores information more effectively if there is an emotional content involved in the activity. The following quotes refer to the joy involved in the games and to the lasting memory of these activities:

> I remember that for me, every time I was in class I was happy. If I were in a bad humor when I went in, I was happy when I came out. I think an energy goes through the whole body—in my body, in my head, in my heart, it seems that it went everywhere.[SM]

> I fell in love with Eurhythmics. My early years, from the time I was a young child, had been filled with so much love for music. Eurhythmics brought this back to me, this musical way of being with music.[RA]

> I hadn't realized that movement was a very personal and joyful form of expression for me. This revelation influenced me then and in years afterward.[CH]

To close this chapter, these inspiring words come from Dominique Porte:

> The Dalcroze method has confirmed the scale of human values I already had and, in addition, has given me the occasion, and the power, to work in harmony with that scale of values. To describe this scale completely would take too long. But starting from the top, I'll just name a few of these values: Truth, liberty, joy, kindness, and inexhaustible beauty of 'to be.'

CHAPTER SEVEN

☙

SHARING THE GIFT

Teaching Eurhythmics

People who want to become Dalcroze teachers must refine their performance skills and their sensitivity in understanding how people function physically, mentally, and emotionally. Learning to design, conduct, and assess class activities demands imagination (to find other ways!), patience, and boundless energy. Teachers must sharpen their own attention and perceptive skills to best facilitate positive changes in the class. Teacher training stresses the symbiotic nature of Dalcroze learning.

The teacher's music and commands instruct the students, and the students' responses communicate to the teacher. The class becomes akin to a jazz improvisation, with the teacher's original plan still forming the backbone (the "bass"). The plan's skeleton becomes embellished with improvisations suggested to the teacher by the manner in which the students perform. As Ruth Alperson of the New York Dalcroze School astutely observes, master Dalcroze teachers' eyes are always fixed on the students.

Imagine being the teacher. It is time to begin the class. You have prepared your "stimulus of the day." You lift your hands to the piano. A musical sound communicates to the students all they need to know. Will you present a truly musical sound combining the best expression of all the elements of dynamic quality, rhythm, nuance, flow, and direction? Unfortunately, a teacher can concentrate so narrowly on one specific element—say, a pattern of a long-short combination—that the improvising is stripped of its joy and becomes a timing exercise of metronomic accuracy rather than a musical presentation of the long-short rhythm. Eventhe simplest of presentations should make the class want to move, even sing along.

You vary the patterns of the improvisation and the activities of the students so that their attention never wavers. You change the pitch, range, tempo, and dynamic level of the commands to break the stream of their expectations. The left hand pattern moves to the right and vice versa.

Calling out instructions while playing, you time the commands so the students hear them at the most advantageous moment to execute a change, neither too early nor too late. If the students are confused, you send another command so they may regain their control and composure. Observing the students' responses, you adjust the music to match their needs. Any serendipitous happenings naturally weave into the fabric of the class.

This should provide some overview of the many elements and tasks a Dalcroze teacher must balance as the class unfolds. Dalcroze realized that the first element in teaching is to present students with a strong sensory message, such as a musical sound or pattern. This sensation stimulates the student's nervous system and travels to the brain. Through experimentation, Dalcroze learned that only when the message is heard clearly is there any possibility of its being heard properly. The teacher's responsibility is to send a clearly perceivable signal. From there, the students learn to focus their attention and refine their behavioral skills. Attention is a skill, and the teacher's task is to expand its limits. If the teacher can concentrate and coordinate multiple activities, he or she can often develop students' attention while expanding their capacity. This is the primary reason why we practice performing canon with arm beats!

An Unusual Dalcroze Exam

Dalcroze took the task of training teachers very seriously. He alone ascertained who had absorbed the essence of his training well enough to carry the designation "Teacher of Eurhythmics." He traveled to training schools in many countries, passing on his work to the advanced students. Laura Campbell of Exeter, England recalls the story of her examination:

> Dalcroze came over in 1938 and gave a special class for the top year. In the middle of the class, there was a long conversation in French between the principal, Miss Long, and Dalcroze. After we finished singing I said, "What did you talk about?" She said he noticed that another girl and I were allowed to go through the program in one year, instead of two. (The other girl had played the piano and I had done some Rhythmics, so Miss Long had allowed us to do the program in one year.) Dalcroze had said, "I didn't see these two last year. Who are they and what are they doing in the third year? You know I never let them do the License in less than two years." His rule had been disobeyed, we should not have been doing the exam. But he was an honest man and at the end of the exam he passed us both. He did not pass any of those who had completed the three years! I like that story because it shows his absolute honesty. After the exam he said he could tell that we both "were there." We knew what the training was about.

"Being there" is not an easily acquired state. It demands the development of musicianship skills, self-awareness, awareness of others' skills and needs, and a great desire to share a continuing growth in the classroom community. This kind of dynamic teaching with energy flowing back and forth between the class and the teacher was Dalcroze's goal. Dalcroze himself put it this way: "A true pedagogue should be at once psychologist, physiologist, and artist. The complete citizen should leave school capable not only of living normally, but of feeling life. He should be in a position both to create and to respond to the creations of others."[1]

Leading and Following: Teachers and Students

The individual students greatly influence how each Dalcroze class develops. An observant teacher makes use of even the tiniest minuscule responses. Once, after experimenting with children for different ways to move, I asked several students to show the class their movement. One shy child, when her turn came, stood frozen while we all waited. I hastily debated how I could avoid embarrassing her by passing her by; or embarrassing her further by taking away her turn by giving a movement of my own; or making the moment into a class crisis by waiting even longer. Then she blinked her eyes. "Oh, what a wonderful movement!" I exclaimed, blinking my eyes rhythmically so that everyone could copy. She felt validated as a contributing student. I was thrilled with what was really a lovely, novel movement! The other children were delighted, blinking away until a new movement was suggested.

A Dalcroze teacher watches for classroom opportunities to let the shy become leaders in non-risky ways and for the bold to take second place without feeling ignored or constrained. The objective is to develop a healthy balance among the dynamic personalities of the class and support each student in what they can give.

Herb Henke pointed out the value of saying, "Do it *with* them" rather than "*watch* so-and-so do it." A shy student is happy to be noticed so long as he or she is not exposed to full scrutiny. A bold child wants the whole stage, and may have it for a moment, but that student also needs to experience the integration of moving as a part of the group. Marjaleena Juntenen notices the value of changing roles with others. "[Dalcroze activities] lessen our fears of being in a group, improve social abilities so we can better work in a group, and help us be either a leader or a follower."

Another respondent describes how her experiences in leading and following helped her overcome her inherent shyness:

> I was always very shy. I was always big and shy of touching. This class made a lot of sense for me. Now I feel more confident. Everything I do is okay. Oh, sometimes I do something wrong—like when I'm on the upbeat and everyone else is on the downbeat. But working together with others, communicating, the leader and follower routine, helps a lot. It doesn't always suit me, but I developed the capacity to do it, even if I don't want to do it at the moment. I have to do it because someone else is depending on me.[SF]

For those who choose Dalcroze teaching as their profession, it becomes a source of true joy. As a young woman, Gabi Chrisman thought she might become a dancer or a concert pianist, not a teacher. However she did become a teacher, largely to show people in Chicago what this "Dalcroze stuff" was. Gabi had her first experience with Dalcroze classes in fifth-grade, in her hometown in Switzerland. Although the classes lasted only one year, they provided her with a lasting impression of great happiness:

> Oh, I loved them, I loved them! I remember one day, we had hoops on the floor and the teacher was at the piano. We had to move through those hoops. (Today I know that we had to do it in time with the music.) That gave me such a sensation. Now teaching it and doing it—it's amazing. Here I am back taking classes in the Grand Salle [in the Jaques-Dalcroze Institute] and I *still* love it. I remember we had to do leaps and skips, and there is nothing more beautiful than skipping to music.

There is an immense satisfaction. Now I understand what I want to do. I want to give that kind of experience, that satisfaction to other people. When people ask me about Dalcroze principles and the goal of training, I always say at the end of my speech: "We seek the harmonization of the human being."

Trust

Trust is one of the most important elements in Dalcroze teaching. Teachers try to establish an atmosphere in which the students feel comfortable in expressing their inner feelings, thoughts, and emotions. As student Fen-Chin remarks: "When I work with good teachers, I can be free. I use some ideas I otherwise might not try. They trust that I could do something, and they don't care about it." Fen-Chin's belief that "they don't care about it" alludes to her observation that the teachers are non-judgmental. The teachers do not give rules about how to move; there are no right or wrong movements, there are only expressive movements.

The teachers strive to instill the classroom with an environment of acceptance so that the students have the freedom to extend their personal boundaries. The Eurhythmics approach develops an increasing awareness of possibilities so students can exercise their artistic judgment about what suits the situation. Fen Chin's "good teachers" encourage their students to experiment, to feel free making music with their bodies in unusual ways. As the students' experience and confidence grow, taste and good judgment grow too. The teacher tailors the music to the needs of the moment, balancing the diverse classroom elements in a well-shaped whole. This building of trust between teachers and students is a vital aspect of Dalcroze work because of the revealing nature of the work:

I think Dalcroze learning is very demanding because you are visible at all times. Your thinking is visible because you are reacting to what you hear with what you understand. Your thoughts are visible and so is your body. I think this is the kind of exposure that many students, especially those who start as adults, find risky. I think it is very important to create an atmosphere in the class of acceptance, patience, and compassion. The teacher tries to enter the world of the student, tries to understand where the student is but does not bring the student into her world. I think that is terribly important, because if students are tense in a Dalcroze class, they won't want to take risks. Then risk-taking will get a bad name, whereas I think we're trying to give a good name to the idea that you can try something you've never done before and give it a whirl.[LP]

A dancer was a participant in one of my summer workshops. She had virtually no knowledge of music, however she was willing to absorb everything. In return she influenced the class with her beautiful movements. My challenge was to couch musical expressions in such a way that she could understand the concepts and make use of them. The nurturing, non-threatening quality of the classes was amply reflected on the last day when she remarked, "It's never felt so good to feel so dumb." Her success in understanding the ideas were made possible in part by the open validating nature of the classroom environment.

Empowerment

As the bond of trust matures between student and teacher, the student's sense of independence grows. Students increasingly feel better equipped to trust their internal resources in successfully dealing with the unknown. Lisa Parker describes how her students gained confidence, learning to trust themselves and to feel the rhythm inside:

The pitfall of Dalcroze teaching is that the teacher can play beautiful music, and the student can lie in the arms of beautiful music, having a marvelous listening experience. But the student may not be empowered to have that music inside them. So we must wean the students, and give them insights so that more and more, everything gets turned over to them. All the music, all the decisions are theirs to make. Then they are really holding the power. They can feel, "Yes, I have the power inside, I don't need you to make the music."

Additional benefits in teaching Eurhythmics are that the teachers share in the growth of their students and continue to experience their own personal expansion. Several Dalcroze teachers revealed that teaching helped them overcome their earlier personal difficulties. Like the students, teachers experience the empowerment of risk-taking: "I was extremely uptight and full of anxiety. In terms of teaching, I've done things I would not have done, gone places I would not have gone—I would have been scared to death."[LP]

Many teachers find increased confidence through their experience in problem solving. The expansion of perceived opportunities is exhilarating and inspiring; one of the tenets of Dalcroze games is that there are numerous solutions to a problem. After we find one solution we are again asked to find another way to accomplish the same task. The persistent request for alternative solutions leads us to believe in our ingenuity in finding other possibilities: All is not lost, find another way.

> I think one of the things that builds confidence in people is that as they begin to develop new ways for approaching an issue, they begin to realize how much of themselves they could be using that they haven't used until now. Once they start to use it, it becomes like new words in a language. They find a wider vocabulary of behavior.[LP]

Sharing in the growth of others and continuing their own path offers immense satisfaction and personal strength: "I was very shy before I came [to America]. Nowadays I can stand before a hundred people I meet in a workshop, at least seventy of whom are music teachers. I learned to stand there and think, do the movement, improvise, and play with ease."MSh This same teacher notes the following changes in her students: "Through Eurhythmics, even non-musicians who feel shy and deficient about their inner musicality gain confidence and strength in their ability to connect wholly to the music."

The Benefits Beyond Music Performance

Dalcroze often referred to the value of training in rhythmic movement before beginning instrumental study:

> Before adapting his nature to the movement and sound of an instrument, the pupil should be capable of experiencing in his body and then analyzing both motor and aural sensations. Special exercises will first develop his sense of muscular rhythm and nervous sensibility, then they will render his ear attentive to all gradations of intensity, duration and time, phrasing and shading, so that his limbs may faithfully reproduce the rhythms perceived by the ear. Hence the pupil will find himself in a better condition for motor receptivity, as well as better prepared to take up studies that aim at converting impression into expression.[2]

Dalcroze also notes the overall benefits of training "in movement and through movement:"

> The aim of [Eurhythmics] is to develop mind and feeling in everything connected with art and life... rhythm and movement are essential factors of every form of art and are indispensable to every thoroughly cultured human being.[3]

Students and teachers alike testify to the enormous power of Eurhythmics. Their experience shows the benefits of studying Eurhythmics are widely applicable to other situations, especially educational situations. In this book Eurhythmics is presented largely in musical terms, both because the authors are musicians and because the studies were conceived in music classes. The essence of the experience, however, is as diverse as life.

> As a basic teaching technology, Dalcroze has incredible strength and can be applied to anything, not just music ... Dalcroze himself was the generalist of all generalists. In teaching literature, I applied Dalcroze teaching for the internal flow, as people do in Solfege and movement when they begin to analyze the music. I tried to get the students to analyze the text, to sense what was going on inside them as they read the text. I wanted them to first temporally get involved with the story and identify with the characters; then move to judging characters. "Have you made a correct decision about whether the character was right or wrong?" I devised exercises to put in practice the Eurhythmics idea of finding the internal flow in this other medium. As I taught in this manner, I was successful. I could get the students to identify with the texts. They had to integrate. The next level of feedback was when I began realizing that what I was doing was indeed authentic because it would work in other people.[AC]

Looking Back and Ahead

We have focused on how Dalcroze's work reveals the way we behave. Recall the three steps that occur with all experience. First something in the environment stimulates our senses: Dalcroze understood the necessity for presenting students with clear, strong sensory images to stimulate the system. Next, the stimulation travels along the nervous system to the brain: Dalcroze ensured the stimulus would receive attention by making small changes to refocus attention and reduce habituation. Finally, the mind compares the stimulus to memories, assesses it, and decides what action to take: Dalcroze measured the success of his work by the quality of the students' overt responses—their behavior.

The sensory system is our valuable source of information, a necessary part of survival; we live in a physical, sensual world, and for our very safety we must be aware. This awareness brings along the possibility of appreciation and joy. To experience these last two, we need to understand the heart and mind. Dalcroze pointed out that the body, mind, and spirit must be in balance. When they are, life is rich.

CHAPTER EIGHT

DALCROZE EXERCISES

Music's elements of time, space, and energy express the essence of the world we live in and provide the stimulus for the exercises in this chapter. There are four principal goals in Eurhythmic exercises:

1. To engage attention and improve concentration

2. To gain mastery of physical movements

3. To find emotional involvement with music

4. To improve communication with others, learning to balance personal needs with the needs of others.

The companion compact disc of Eurhythmics exercises presents a unique opportunity in the current Dalcroze literature to study and experience the timing of commands. (The written commands in the text of Chapter 8 are the same as those spoken on the CD.) As we discussed in Chapter 2, it is vital for the teacher's commands to be clear, rhythmic, and coordinated with the music. The accompanying CD provides a format for you to experiment with this approach.

The following exercises should be done in order; each exercise builds on the previous one. Your concentration will increase as you become more aware of your muscular sensations. Note how various groups of muscles pull and relax. Feel the weight of your body as you shift, lean forward, hold still, pull against and are pulled by gravity. Appreciate your growing sense of balance as it improves with each exercise, regardless of how passive or active the movement.

Listen to the messages of your proprioceptive system so that you can improve activities you engage in frequently. Moving through ordinary activities with fluidity saves strain on the body; the sensation of moving efficiently is pleasurable. Accomplished athletes always convey the impression that what they are doing is easy; power flows through their movements to its intended conclusion without the impediments of unnecessary tension.

Before you begin an exercise, read through the instructions; then listen to the CD and follow along. After finishing an exercise, write your own observations and experiences in a notebook or journal. Then read the discussion of the exercise. After considering the ideas presented, perform the exercise again. Be sure to make notes each time you complete an exercise.

EXERCISE 1: WARM-UP

Focus: weight, gravity, tension, and relaxation

Dalcroze classes usually begin with some preliminary movement work. These exercises increase our awareness of how flexible the body can be. They help us focus on the sensations of movement and breathing. During this preliminary work, music provides flow, continuity, and expressiveness, thereby heightening our emotional involvement.

Preparation: Read all the instructions before beginning the CD with track 1.

1. Assume a quiet standing position. (You should feel relaxed; not straining to maintain the position.)

2. Close your eyes.

3. Notice your breathing; do not attempt to change it in any way.

4. Breathe deeply into your upper chest and let it go easily.

5. Breathe into your abdomen, feel it expand, and let the breath go.

6. Lift one arm slowly toward the ceiling and let it return. Now lift the other and let it return.

7. Lift the forearm a short distance and let it fall. Repeat with the other.

8. Bend one wrist, then release. Now the other.

9. Lift the thumb on one hand, and release. Then the other.

10. Lift each finger one after the other. Now the other hand.

11. Lift one shoulder toward the ceiling and let it relax. Repeat with the other shoulder.

12. Leaving arms and shoulders at your sides, rotate one elbow toward the front and let it relax. Repeat with the other elbow.

13. Lower your head almost to your chest. Gradually lift it to rest above the spinal column.

14. Slowly turn you head to one side, looking over your shoulder. Now in the other direction.

15. Slowly move your right ear toward your right shoulder without letting your shoulders move. Then left ear to left shoulder.

16. Move the midriff away from the spine, then relax.

17. Move the spine away from the midriff, and relax.

18. Move one hip as if you were trying to touch your shoulder, then relax. Move the other hip towards the shoulder, and relax.

19. Tilt the pelvis forward, relax, then backward, and relax.

20. Lift one knee, extend the leg and return. Now lift the other knee and extend the leg, and return.

21. Lift the heel so the knee is slightly bent and move the knee out to one side. Return. Repeat with the other leg.

22. Keeping the heel on the floor, lift the foot and relax. Repeat with the other foot.

23. Curl all the toes on one foot. Relax. Repeat with the other foot.

24. Then try moving each toe separately. First on one foot, then the other.

25. Write down your observations.

Observations and Questions for Exercise 1

Notice the tempo of inhalation and exhalation. Note the location of movement in your chest and abdomen. Do not look at your body's movements—feel them from inside where they are occurring.

As you move, notice the effect of gravity on your body. Feel the difference between using your own energy to move and letting gravity move you.

Concentrate on sensing muscle movement. Where do you feel the muscle pulling that moves a particular body part against gravity?

Notice at what point your muscles have to stretch.

Check other parts of the body. Are your knees, ankles, or back tense? Let them relax and monitor them as you move.

Notice the different sensations in body involvement: the shift in weight, muscle activity, joint functioning, even in slight excitations.

Now repeat Exercise 1 being more conscious of your sensations.

EXERCISE 2: LABAN EFFORT ACTIONS

Focus: motor control and sensitivity to images

The following exercises will expand upon the movements we have learned in Exercise 1 by adding a variety of qualities. The English stage director Rudolf Laban (who created this exercise) organized the relationships of weight, time, and space into a system of gestures called eight basic effort actions.

He designates two of these effort actions, thrusting and floating, as the principal movements. The other movements are derived by altering one of the parameters of weight (W), time (T), and space (S). A change in weight involves a shift from gentle to firm; a change in time, from sudden to sustained; and a change in space, from direct to flexible.

Thrusting
(WEIGHT=FIRM, TIME=SUDDEN, SPACE=DIRECT)

Dabbing
(W=GENTLE, T=SUDDEN, S=DIRECT)

Pressing
(W=FIRM, T=SUSTAINED, S=DIRECT)

Slashing
(W=FIRM, T=SUDDEN, S=FLEXIBLE)

Floating
(W=GENTLE, T=SUSTAINED, S=FLEXIBLE)

Wringing
(W=FIRM, T=SUSTAINED, S=FLEXIBLE)

Flicking
(W=GENTLE, T=SUDDEN, S=FLEXIBLE)

Gliding
(W=GENTLE, T=SUSTAINED, S=DIRECT)

Preparation: Begin Track 2 of the CD. Assume a standing position.

1. Thrust: Move one leg from bent to straight with a thrust, like thrusting a shovel into the ground. Change to the other leg. Alternate legs.

2. Dab: Lift a finger and make a dab, like dabbing sunscreen on yourself.

3. Press: Imagine pressing the lower back into clay. Press. Release. Press. Release. Longer Press.

4. Slash: With your arm as a sword, slash the letter Z in the air. Now use the other arm.

5. Float: Let both arms float like seaweed on the waves.

6. Wring: Use both hands to wring out a wet cloth.

7. Flick: Flick at tiny bread crumbs.

8. Glide: Gently glide just the midriff forward and back, as is it was a drawer.

9. Write down your observations.

Observations and Questions for Exercise 2

Recall the movements and be aware of how your muscles felt. Which movements were suitable for you? Which were not? Devise some movements of your own according to Laban's classifications.

Imagine that movements generate sound and expression. Close your eyes and allow other parts of your body to become involved in the movement so that there is complete body experience of the patterns.

Repeat the exercise and be aware of how your gestures and the music fit together.

EXERCISE 3: MOVE THE BEAT TO A DIFFERENT PLACE

Focus: alertness and motor control

Preparation: Begin the CD track for Exercise 3. Assume a standing position.

1. Listen. Clap your hands to match the beat. (Clap in circles with just the fingertips. Concentrate on the space between the claps.)

2. Move your shoulders to the beat.

3. In the hips.

4. In one foot. In the other foot

5. In the head

6. In another place.

7. In the knees.

8. Take a walk.

9. And stop.

10. Write down your observations.

Observations and Questions for Exercise 3

Recall the space these different movements occupied. Which were largest? Which did you find most comfortable? The least comfortable? Which movement required the most energy? The least energy? Describe these movements according to Laban's terms. (More than one answer is possible.) Recall the changes in quality of sound—did you change the quality of your movement to match?

Did you hear a change in the tempo (speed) of the music? Be alert. Follow the changes by continuously adjusting your steps to the music's beat.

Did you notice a change in dynamics (the loud or soft dimension of music)? Try changing the amount of energy going into your feet as you step.

Repeat the exercise, being more aware of all the dimensions of the music and your movement.

This exercise helps improve the capacity to react quickly and appropriately to the quality of the sounds. Try not to anticipate or hesitate at the commands. Imagine letting the body react before the brain. As your skill increases, you will become more attentive not just to the initial sound of the musical cue but also to the length and the dynamic of the music. Try utilizing this skill during other situations. For example, while another person is speaking, concentrate on the whole message in the same way that you concentrated on the whole movement from beginning to end in this exercise. Be aware of the movements other people make while they speak.

When listening to artists perform, see if they remain focused throughout the length of a note. A great singer will "color" each note letting it add its own moment of life to the whole design. The degree of expression—the control of energy—becomes more and more evident as you listen with concentration to the length of the music.

EXERCISE 4: FORWARD AND BACKWARD

Focus: aural concentration, motor control, and timing

Preparation: Begin the CD track for Exercise 4. Assume a standing position and practice walking forward and backward.

1. Listen.

2. Take a step on every sound.

3. When you hear "change" walk backwards. Change.

4. When you hear "change" again walk forward. Change.

5. Alternate each time you hear "change."

6. And stop.

7. Write your observations.

Observations and Questions for Exercise 4

Observe yourself and notice when your attention level is lagging. Going in a circle may become very dull so make your pathway interesting. Try walking figure eights, or the pattern of a Yin/Yang symbol, or a spiral.

The goal in this exercise is to make the change without missing a beat. Your response should be smooth and quick. At first you may find yourself walking stiffly, tense with the expectation of a change signal at any moment. You should move easily, as if you were going to do this forever and enjoy it all the way. The mind, however, should be alert, ready to hear the signal and command the body's movement. If the body is moving in an easy smooth way it will shift easily. If your body's response is jerky or out of balance, you may be holding tension in areas of the body not required for walking. Check your shoulders, elbows, and wrists. We often tense these joints when they are not needed for the immediate movement. Give them a rest!

Eventually alertness will come with a sense of ease, not tenseness. Enjoy what you are doing, knowing that you can change quickly, easily, and accurately. Repeat this exercise and incorporate these observations.

The body-mind goal is to have the stimulus of the verbal or musical command go from the ear to the brain and be understood and acted upon quickly and accurately with no interference of the flow of activity.

EXERCISE 5: SOUND AND SILENCE—FOLLOW

Focus: imaging of durations, inner hearing, inhibition

Preparation: Begin the CD track for Exercise 5. Assume a standing position.

1. Listen. Tap the beat.

2. When the music stops, you stop.

3. Show the beat a different way.

4. Show the beat another way.

5. While the music plays, stop and listen.

6. When the music stops, show the beat.

7. When the music stops, count the beats.

8. And count: 1, 2, 3, 4.

9. Walk with the music.

10. When the music stops, stop and count silently.

11. And stop.

12. Write down your observations.

Observations and Questions for Exercise 5

Were you able to change to different groups of counting? Did you tense up in anticipation of the stops? Did you move even slightly on the silent pulses? What were your feelings when the music came earlier or later than you expected?

When you repeat this exercise try to remain focused but calm, releasing any tensions you feel. You should be thoroughly relaxed when you are not moving. Check your knees, shoulder, head, and elbows and keep them loose.

EXERCISE 6: DRAWER PULL—INTERNALIZING

Focus: imaging of space and motor-memory

Preparation: Imagine pulling open a drawer and then pushing it shut. Do this with one arm. Begin Track 6 on the CD.

1. Now listen to the music.

2. Pull and push.

3. With the other arm.

4. And both arms.

5. Close your eyes and continue the movements.

6. Imagine the movements while the music goes on.

7. When the music stops continue to imagine the motions.

8. Now make the motions.

9. And stop.

10. Write down your observations.

Observations and Questions for Exercise 6

How strong was your impression of the motions? Do you remember details such as the color and texture of the drawer, the temperature, odor, and warmth of its surface. What were your sensations of muscle effort and eye movement. When you repeat the exercise, see if your senses of touch, sound, and movement are more vivid than on your first trial. Pay extra attention to the angles in the shoulders, wrists, and elbows. Notice the muscle sensations when you shift from push to pull.

When the music became louder did you use more energy, pulling the drawer farther out? When the music was at its loudest, what parts of the body became involved?

EXERCISE 7: PHRASING—QUICK RESPONSE AND FOLLOW

Focus: attention, time and space, and motor control

Preparation: Begin the CD track for Exercise 7. Assume a seated position.

1. Lean slowly to one side.

2. Lean another way.

3. Change.

4. Longer now.

5. The music will tell you.

6. Write down your observations.

Observations and Questions for Exercise 7

Did you feel the connection between your feet and the floor? Did you feel your weight balanced between your feet and your hips? buttocks? sit-bones? Did you run out of space when leaning? Be very aware of your weight distribution and sense how it shifts from one side to the other.

Notice what happens to your center of balance. Which muscles are most used? What is the shape of your back? Did it remain straight or did it bend? Feel your backbone as the center of your whole torso and let it explore space as one unit. See if this improves your sensation of balance and connection to the floor.

EXERCISE 8: COCKTAIL PIANO—QUICK REACTION

Focus: attention, motor control, improvisation, imagination

Preparation: Begin the CD track for Exercise 8. Assume a seated position.

1. Listen.

2. As the music plays, show the beat.

3. Put it somewhere else.

4. Imagine the beat.

5. When the music stops, clap the beats.

6. Snap the beat.

7. In the feet.

8. Pretend you're at the piano

9. When the music stops, take a solo.

10. My turn!

11. Write down your observations.

Observations and Questions for Exercise 8

What was the quality of beat according to the Laban effort actions? Were you able to fill in all the silent beats? What parts of the body seemed appropriate for showing the beat? When you do this exercise again, try showing the beat with other parts of the body.

Were you anticipating or hesitating at solo entrances? Were you surprised by the long solos? Did you feel you were going to run out of ideas? Enjoy the unexpected moments.

EXERCISE 9: TWICE AS FAST AND TWICE AS SLOW

Focus: attention, motor control, energy, imagination

Preparation: Begin the CD track for Exercise 9. Assume a standing position for walking.

1. Listen.

2. Step to the beat.

3. Slower steps. (third beat)

4. Return.

5. Faster. (fourth beat)

6. Return.

7. Now the music will tell you.

8. And stop.

9. Write your observations.

Observations and Questions for Exercise 9

Were you able to adjust from one speed to another smoothly? Did you stay balanced? Think about the length of your steps. Did they change with the music—longer with the slower beats and shorter with the faster beats? How did your shoulders move at the changes? Did you also change the direction of your walking when you changed speed? This is not necessary; just an interesting possibility. Recall how your feet meet the floor during each speed. Was there a difference? Experiment with keeping the same foot position (either flat, a strong toe-roll, or tip-toe) throughout the different speeds and see how each feels.

Transitions are always the hard spots to control. When you repeat this exercise be prepared to shift your flow of energy quickly at the changes. Repeat this exercise with clapping, with changing body taps to different locations, and any other movements you can think of that let you go twice as fast and twice as slow.

EXERCISE 10: FLICK AND GLIDE

Focus: energy control, direction, weight, motor control

Preparation: Begin the CD track for Exercise 10. Assume a standing position.

1. Listen.

2. Find a movement for the music you hear. This is Movement 1.

3. Find a new way. Find a new way. And stop.

4. Listen.

5. Find a movement for the new music. This is Movement 2.

6. Find a new way.

7. Put this Movement in your feet.

8. When the music tells you, add Movement 1 in your hands.

9. Write down your observations.

Observations and Questions for Exercise 10

Which of the Laban effort actions do you feel was aroused by the music? Which body movements felt most appropriate for the music you heard? Were you able to add Movement 1 to Movement 2? Did you do this smoothly? Did you notice that the Movement 1 music sometimes stopped while Movement 2 continued? Did you stop your hand movements to match the music?

This is a complex exercise demanding intense concentration. You must coordinate two movements of different qualities while starting and stopping one of the movements. As you repeat the exercise focus on stopping and starting Movement 1 exactly with the musical cues. As an even more challenging experiment, try starting and stopping the other movement at times of your own choosing.

EXERCISE 11: STATUES

Focus: concentration, motor control, organization,
movement, improvisation

Preparation: Begin the CD track for Exercise 11 and assume a standing position.

1. Listen, count the beats in groups of four "1-2-3-4."

2. When you say "1," change your position.

3. Now change on 3.

4. Keep counting!

5. Now change on 2.

6. Now change on 4.

7. Now change on 4 and 1.

8. Now 1 and 3.

9. Now on 2 and 3.

10. Now on 2 and 4.

11. Now 1, 2 and 3.

12. Now all the beats.

13. And stop.

14. Write down your observations.

Observations and Questions for Exercise 11

Were you able to count while moving? Did your movements vary? Did they change according to which beats they came on? Could you make your changes at the right time?

Repeat the exercise. Be sure to vary your movements by feeling the energy in the musical beat.

EXERCISE 12: INTERFERENCE

Focus: concentration, beat memory (aural and muscular)

Preparation: Begin track 12 on the CD. Be prepared to walk to the beat.

1. Listen to the beat.

2. Ready, walk.

3. When the music stops, keep on walking.

4. And walk, no matter what you hear. Keep walking.

5. Stop walking and think the beat.

6. Be very still.

7. Step the beat.

8. And stop.

9. Write down your observations.

Observations and Questions for Exercise 12

This exercise demands that you maintain an inner sense of the movement's energy and regularity while hearing a different musical impulse. Were you able to maintain your sense of walking while unexpected and uncooperative music interfered? Did you maintain your movement when actually walking and then continue to feel the sensation in your imagination? This is a profound test of your ability to channel several streams of information at once. Success comes only by focusing on the sensations of your whole body moving, by internalizing your awareness of the rhythmic flow.

EXERCISE 13: CHANGING METER

Focus: awareness of habituation and change, perception
of contrast and body control, varying levels of energy, accent,
internalization, proprioceptive memory, combining of
several movements and activities.

Optional: Use an object that resonates and something to strike it with—such as a pan lid and a pencil. Check all your lids to find the one that is the most musical.

Preparation: Begin the CD track for Exercise 13. Assume a standing position.

1. Listen. Count the beats in groups of four, "1-2-3-4."

2. Step on every count.

3. Tap somewhere when you say "1." (You may also try using an object or clapping hands.)

4. Count the beats in groups of three, "1-2 -3." Be sure to tap on 1.

5. Go back to four, "1-2-3-4."

6. Change to 3.

7. Now groups of 2.

8. 3 now.

9. And 4

10. Write down your observations.

Observations and Questions for Exercise 13

This exercise demands both concentration and relaxation to get into the swing of the music. Were your knees relaxed at the stop?

Were your elbows relaxed while you clapped? Keep your claps gentle and circular, your footsteps light and gliding.

Music's meter is the measurement of the flow of pulses into groups. Most music adheres to a single meter throughout. A waltz is in 3-meter. A march is in 2- or 4-meter. However some music changes meter, either between large sections of a composition, or often as part of the basic rhythmic organization. Music from such countries as Greece, Turkey, and Bulgaria often combines two meters to match dance steps.

EXERCISE 14: ECHO (INTERRUPTED CANON)

Focus: concentration, memory, motor control

This exercise uses silent clapping—clapping without touching hands.

Preparation: Begin the CD track for Exercise 14. Assume a standing position.

1. Listen. Clap the pattern.

2. Put it somewhere else. And somewhere else.

3. Get ready to step the next pattern.

4. Step.

5. Write down your observations.

Observations and Questions for Exercise 14

Did you respond to every phrase? Were you in phase with the rhythm or did you come in too early? It is important to feel and move with the swing of the rhythm. Check for tension in your elbow and knee joints. You should be at ease and ready to respond with a smooth flow, neither rushed nor stiff.

How was your echoing skill? Are you confident that you echoed the phrases accurately? Did your memory include not only the correct durations but also a feel of the dynamics and direction of the music? Did you show the flow of the music with some beats a bit louder than others and the last note of each pattern usually soft? When you repeat the exercise listen carefully for the quality of the phrases and aim for that quality in your response. Let your body respond directly to the music and resist the temptation to "get it" intellectually.

Do this exercise again and find new places to clap. Use more flexibility in your movements. Later try this exercise with walking all the patterns instead of starting with silent clapping.

EXERCISE 15: TRUE CANON

Focus: concentration, divided attention

Preparation: Begin the CD track for Exercise 15. Assume a standing position.

I'll play a pattern, you step 4 counts after me. Here's an example.

1. Get ready to step.

2. Listen. Step what you've heard.

3. Write down your observations.

Observations and Questions for Exercise

Were you able to continue to the end? This is the most difficult of all the exercises. Do not feel distressed if you lost your way or felt uncertain. Canon demands total concentration, keen attention to musical sounds, and excellent motor control. Just as in Exercise 12 (Interference) you must retain a musical sensation and express it in your movement while you are hearing a different sound. Unlike Exercise 12 you must pay attention to the different sound because this is the next pattern you will move!

Imagine the body can think on its own. Shut off as much mental interference as possible. Let the body experience the music first. Try to achieve a subconscious feeling of flow, free from excess tension and crippling thoughts. Let the body respond directly to the music and avoid processing the exercise intellectually. Go with the flow!

Repeat the exercise many times. Eventually you will know the patterns and can enjoy the pleasure of feeling your movements cooperate with the music. At this point the exercise no longer demands the same intense concentration as when you began. To keep up the challenge have someone devise new canons for you to follow!

Work in canon gives the musician an understanding of counterpoint and fugue. For the rest of us, this training helps us deal with the myriad of demands each day brings. We can process more information, fewer details are missed, and our concentration expands.

EXERCISES FOR MORE THAN ONE

All the exercises presented can be done with a partner or a small group. Sharing encouragement and personal observations can contribute to success of the exercises. Mark Twain said, "To get the full value of joy, you must have someone to divide it with."

APPENDIX

List of interview respondents, in order of first initial

AA–Anait Aroustamian, Russia

AB–Anna Baker, Poland, USA

AC–Abbott Chrisman, USA,
　　Switzerland

AD–Alexandra Dalton, England

AM–Alice Moseley, Scotland

AS– Anita Stevens, England

BI–Barbara Imbrie, USA

BM–Benina Mulder, Holland

BPH–Beatrice Perlman Hodel, USA

CA–Charles Aschbrenner, USA

CH–Charlotte Hubert, USA

CMM–Carmen Martin Moreno, Spain

DP–Dominique Porte, Switzerland

FCL–Fan–Chin Lin, Taiwan

GC–Gabi Chrisman, Switzerland

HH–Herbert Henke, USA

HvM–Hettie von Maanen, Holland

JEK–Joy E. Kane, USA, France

JLAP–Jose Luis Arostegui Plaza, Spain

KG–Karin Greenhead, England

KI–Karla Isenberg, USA

KW–Karen Williams, USA

LM–Louise Milota, USA

LP–Lisa Parker, USA

LR–Lena Romanov, Russia

MB–Margaret Brink, USA

MLB–Marie–Laure Bachmann,
　　Switzerland

MHA–Malou Hatt-Arnold,
　　Switzerland

MJ–MarjaLeena Juntunen. Finland

MSh–Mindy Shieh, Taiwan

MSz–Marta Sanchez, USA

PH–Patricia Holmes, Australia

RA–Ruth Alperson, USA

SF–Shulamith Feingold, Israel

SMc–Susan McCarthy, USA

SM–Sylvie Morgenegg. Switzerland

SN–Sandra Nash, Australia

TeB–Terry Boyarsky, USA

ToB–Tomoko Bouvier, Japan, France

UH–Ulla Hellquist. Sweden

VM–Virginia Mead, USA

ENDNOTES

CHAPTER 1

1. Jaques-Dalcroze, Emile. *Notes Bariolles,* (Geneva: J.H. Jeheber, 1948), 22.

2. Ibid., 195

3. Berchtold, Alfred. "Emile Jaques-Dalcroze et son temps," in *Emile Jaques-Dalcroze, L'Homme, Le Compositeur, Le Createur de la Ryhthmique,* ed. Frank Martin, (Neuchetel: La Baconniere, 1965), 40.

4. Jaques-Dalcroze, Emile. *La Musique et Nous,* (Geneva: Perret-Gentil, 1945), 143-144.

5. Ibid., 87

6. Ibid., 140

7. Jaques-Dalcroze, *Notes Bariolles*

8. Jaques-Dalcroze, Emile. *Rhythm, Music, and Education,* trans. by H.F. Rubinstein, (Redcourt, England: The Dalcroze Society), viii.

9. Weiss, Piero and Richard Taruskin. *Music of the Western World,* (New York: Schirmer Books, 1984), 8.

10. Jaques-Dalcroze, Emile. *Eurhythmics, Art, and Education,* trans. by Frederick Rochwell, (New York: Arno Press, 1976), 59.

CHAPTER 2

1. H'doubler, Maragaret N. "Movement and Its Rhythmic Structure," unpublished paper, (University of Wisconsin, 1946) 1.

2. The trampoline is a musical instrument! I keep one under my grand piano and use it regularly. Bouncing is not only fun, it makes people aware of how body energy is related to space. It also establishes a steady beat, even with people who have an awkward and irregular gait. While they bounce, they can also clap hands or tap a drum to match the bounce, or they can change patterns, such as tapping only every other bounce or twice on each bounce. Infinite variations are possible.

3. Jaques-Dalcroze, Emile. *Rhythm, Music, and Education,* (Redcourt, England: The Dalcroze Society 1967), 97.

4. Jaques-Dalcroze, Emile. *Eurhythmics, Art, and Education,* 59.

5. Ibid., 246.

CHAPTER 3

1. Hirst, William. "The Psychology of Attention," in *Mind and Brain: Dialogues in Cognitive Neuroscience,* ed. James Le Doux and William Hirst, (Cambridge: Cambridge University Press, 1986), 113.

2. Moray, Neville. *Listening and Attention,* (Baltimore: Penguin Books, 1969), 90.

3. Becknell, Arthur F., Jr. "A History of the Development of Dalcroze Eurhythmics in the United States and Its Influence on the Public School Music Program," (unpublished dissertation, University of Michigan, 1970), 28.

CHAPTER 4

1. Hirst, William. "The Psychology of Attention," in *Mind and Brain: Dialogues in Cognitive Neuroscience,* ed. James Le Doux and William Hirst, (Cambridge: Cambridge University Press, 1986), 122-123.

2. Ibid., 126, 135.

3. Ibid., 129.

4. Jones, Mari Reiss. "Time, our last dimension: Toward a new theory of perception, attention, and memory," in *Psychological Review,* (1976: 83; 5) 323-355.

CHAPTER 5

1. Lindsay and Norman. *Human Information Processing,* (New York: Academic Press, 1972), 381.

2. Delacour, J. "Introduction: The Memory System of the Brain," in *The Memory System of the Brain,* ed. J. Delacour, (Singapore: World Scientific Publishing Co., 1994), 5.

3. Schacter, Daniel. *Searching for Memory,* (New York: Harper-Collins, 1996), 45.

4. Markowitsch, Hans. "Effects of Emotion and Arousal on Memory Processing by the Brain," in *Memory System of the Brain,* 218.

5. Ibid., 227, 212.

6. Delacour, *Memory System of the Brain,* 39.

7. Jaques-Dalcroze, Emile. *Eurhythmics, Art, and Education,* 65.

8. Jaques-Dalcroze, Emile. *Rhythm, Music, and Education,* 55.

9. Macdonald, Heinber, Frueling, and Meredith. "Generating Alternatives," in *Psychological Report,* (1976: 38), 67-72.

10. Jaques-Dalcroze, *Eurhythmics, Art, and Education,* 59.

CHAPTER 6

1. Goleman, Daniel. *Emotional Intelligence,* (New York: Bantam, 1995), 263.

2. Restle, Frank. "Serial Patterns: Their Role in Processing," in *Journal of Experimental Psychology,* (1972: 94a), 299-307.

3. Jaques-Dalcroze, Emile. *Rhythm, Music, and Education,* 98.

4. Ibid., 99.

5. Goleman, Daniel. *Emotional Intelligence,* 145-146.

CHAPTER 7

1. Jaques-Dalcroze, Emile. *Eurhythmics, Art, and Education,* 59.

2. Ibid., p. 106.

3. Ibid., p. 102